Wellness City

Ari-Veikko Anttiroiko

Wellness City

Health and Well-being in Urban Economic Development

palgrave
macmillan

Ari-Veikko Anttiroiko
Faculty of Management
University of Tampere
Tampere, Finland

ISBN 978-3-319-75561-8 ISBN 978-3-319-75562-5 (eBook)
https://doi.org/10.1007/978-3-319-75562-5

Library of Congress Control Number: 2018935832

Cover illustration: Abstract Bricks and Shadows © Stephen Bonk/Fotolia.co.uk

Printed on acid-free paper

This Palgrave Pivot imprint is published by the registered company Springer International Publishing AG part of Springer Nature.
The registered company address is: Gewerbestrasse 11, 6330 Cham, Switzerland

To my beloved son, Pauli.

Contents

List of Figures

CHAPTER 1

Introduction

Abstract This chapter introduces the idea of a wellness city and outlines the structure of the book. Discussion revolves around wellness-oriented urban economic development anchored in the holistic idea of wellness, which reflects people striving for bodily, mental, and spiritual health. The rapid rise of both wellness-promoting lifestyles and wellness industries as significant economic factors are irrefutable signs of the increased importance of wellness in urban economies. For this reason, local governments have gradually started to place wellness on their economic development agendas. Indeed, a wellness city has become a new strategic option for urban economic development on a par with such concepts as a high-tech city or a creative city.

Keywords Wellness • Health • Urban • City • Wellness city • Wellness economy

This book discusses the promotion of wellness-oriented urban economic development. Wellness is a holistic view of personal health-promoting attitudes and actions. For some decades it has been mainly associated with spas, fitness, beauty products and treatments, healthy nutrition, alternative medicine, and meditation. A particularly strong association with the spa economy has kept it, to a degree, on the margins of local economic development policy.

A.-V. Anttiroiko, *Wellness City*,
https://doi.org/10.1007/978-3-319-75562-5_1

Indeed, in previous decades, wellness may not have looked like a particularly viable option for local politicians, public managers, or developers, when compared with high-tech, advanced business services, or creative industries. This is rooted in the view of wellness as a low-paid and low-skill sector, but it is biased in some important respects. In short, business boosted by the rising global lifestyle and wellness trends is expanding and diversifying, and it seems that the time is ripe for integrating it into the local economic development agenda.

A wellness cluster as a geographic concentration of interconnected companies and institutions that contribute to wellness business has an indirect impact on the overall atmosphere, image, and vitality of a city. Its businesses generally have a low barrier to entry and in many fields it employs people who cannot be employed by companies that require university degrees or high-level technical skills. It also has a much stronger connection with the locality than many other industries. However, it is important to keep in mind that the wellness industry has another side that encompasses technology, knowledge, and know-how intensive high value-added activities. For a particular paradigmatic reason, *wellness discourse* has tended to downplay the medical, scientific, and technological aspects of the wellness economy, but this is about to change and take it in new directions.

A particular interest here is the uniquely integrative nature of wellness and its ability to perform "patching" in urban economic development. It is a growing global business with established industries and several high value-added segments, at the same time it plays a special supportive role in locality development by forming an important part of urban amenities and by bringing homegrown elements into the picture through traditional healing, local food, local natural assets, local culture, and spiritual traditions. It adds an authentic flavor when attracting capital, talent, businesses, and visitors to the locality.

A conditioning factor worth taking into account when assessing the significance of wellness for urban economic development is the emergence of a post-industrial economy, a contextual factor behind the economic restructuring that swept through the advanced industrial economies after World War II. This refers essentially to the loss of industrial production to low-cost countries and the higher reliance on high-tech and services. It is a statistical fact that in many industrialized countries manufacturing has been declining for decades while services have increased their relative importance. This spurs the rise of urban wellness and connects it with such fundamental issues as service innovation, integration, and transformation (Nielsen et al. 2013).

Another setting for wellness discourse is the development of modern health care systems. Something interesting is happening in this respect, for public health care systems are being reformed throughout the Western world due to harmful bureaucratic features, legitimation crises, effectiveness problems, increasing demand, and rising costs. Health care reforms are accompanied by the increased role of both preventive care and public health within the health care sector, which increases business opportunities at various points of the "health continuum" (Kickbusch and Payne 2003). What seems to be happening is the transformation of major hospital districts into health care hubs with medical schools, life science research, and medical industries at their core; at the same time wellness centers with varying profiles—from sauna and massage to fitness to meditation—have surged as holistic health destinations. They are becoming closer to each other as the medical paradigm is aligning with prevention and public health, and the wellness paradigm is becoming more evidence-based and sophisticated with the help of new technologies.

A background factor worth a special mention is the dramatic change in the scope and volumes of *wellness businesses*. Modern wellness businesses gained currency in the post-war decades and started to diversify in the 1970s. Among the early signs of the approaching revolution were the establishment of destinations like Canyon Ranch health resort in Tucson, Arizona, in 1979. The business expanded in the 1990s and 2000s due to a lifestyle-related demand for wellness products, services, events, and activity environments. A related boost came from technological advancements that created new business opportunities in this sector. Paul Pilzer (2007) was among the first to popularize the rise of wellness as "the next trillion dollar industry." In 2007, *The Economist* (January 4, 2007) published an article with the title "The wellness boom: Helping consumers to lead healthy lifestyles is becoming a big business." Around the same time, health care hubs and wellness research centers became visible parts of urban development (e.g. Blankenhorn 2010). A few years later *The Huffington Post* published a story that claimed the mid-2010s was the time when businesses became aware of the benefits of workplace wellness (Huffington 2015). All such news stories were signs of the rapid expansion of the wellness industry, which by the mid-2010s had grown to be a market of some USD 3.7 trillion, and at a faster pace than the global economy as a whole (Global Wellness Institute 2017).

A fundamental factor behind the wellness revolution was an increased awareness of problems with a modern hectic and consumption-dominated lifestyle, which triggered the search for new health-conscious values, lifestyles, and methods. Wellness-oriented lifestyles are particularly appealing to well-educated people with a high income, which is a special incentive to the business community (Dvorak et al. 2014). However, the mainstream trend is accompanied by the alternative views of a younger generation fascinated by sharing, downshifting, mindfulness, slow living, and sustainability. It addresses such issues as threats to environmental resilience, lack of fairness in society, and institutions' widespread failures to show social responsibility. There are thus two paths for the demand-driven wellness surge: the mainstream wellness trend that feeds health care and wellness businesses; and the margins that generate niches of lifestyle, sharing, communal, and confessional economies.

Urban governments, developers, and business owners have recognized these market developments. That is why traditional wellness destinations are nowadays accompanied by a range of new wellness communities, health care hubs, and urban wellness centers. It is the reason for cities such as Mitsuke, Tampere, Sendai, Austin, Las Vegas, or Detroit, and regions and city-states such as Dubai, Jeju island, or Napa Valley, to utilize wellness in their promotion and economic development policies. An inevitable outcome of this development is that health and wellness industries are reshaping both suburbs and inner-city areas and are becoming integral parts of urban revitalization. They have an inherent connection with local assets and through them to locality development, the latter due to varying locality-specific advantages, be it the exceptional beauty of local landscapes, hot springs, local food cultures, traditional healing, clustering of wellness businesses, spiritual traditions, or something else. In general, even if delocalization and disembedding mechanisms are at work in wellness, as they are in any area of modern life, wellness has deep roots in the life of local communities.

Wellness is approached in this book in a holistic way, as understood in the classic three-fold concept of bodily, mental, and spiritual health (Dunn 1959). A wellness city, in turn, is a city that supports such aspects of life in an urban community and utilizes them in local development policy. This approach brings together three conceptual pillars, as depicted in Fig. 1.1, on which this book is built: wellness or holistic health and well-being; economic development; and urban communities.

This book starts with a conceptual clarification, proceeds to the role of wellness in economic development, and ends with societal aspects of such developments. Chapter 2 discusses the semantic field associated with well-

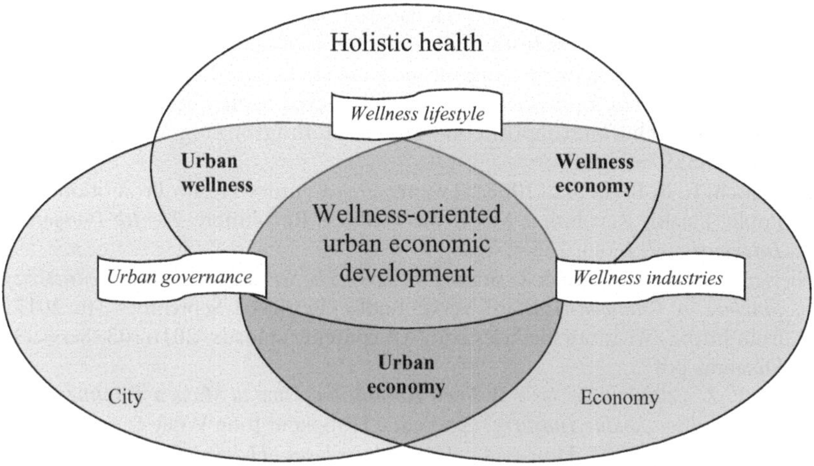

Fig. 1.1 Three pillars of the wellness city

ness and clarifies the major dimensions of the core concepts of this field. Chapter 3 drills deeper into the urban dimension of wellness, providing a particular context to the discussion. Chapter 4 provides a general introduction to the role of wellness in local economic development, while Chap. 5 takes the discussion further on the basis of the major dimensions of wellness. Chapter 6 brings forth examples of the building of health care and wellness cities, representing cases of community, tourism, and high-tech oriented strategies. Chapter 7 contextualizes the wellness issue by highlighting the benefits of a wellness for all paradigm for local economic development. The last chapter briefly summarizes the core message of the book and encapsulates the main findings.

References

Blankenhorn, D. (2010, September 22). The Wellness Research Center Boom. *DZNet*. Retrieved September 17, 2017, from http://www.zdnet.com/article/the-wellness-research-center-boom/

Dunn, H. L. (1959). High-Level Wellness for Man and Society. *American Journal of Public Health, 49*(6), 786–792.

Dvorak, D., Saari, S., & Tuominen, T. (Eds.). (2014). *Developing a Competitive Health and Well-being Destination*. Turku: Turku University of Applied Sciences.

Global Wellness Institute. (2017, January). *Global Wellness Economy Monitor*. Miami: Global Wellness Institute.

Huffington, A. (2015, July 5). Big Business Finally Learns that Wellness Is Good Business. *The Huffington Post, The Blog*. Retrieved September 17, 2017, from http://www.huffingtonpost.com/arianna-huffington/big-business-finally-lear_b_5559758.html

Kickbusch, I., & Payne, L. (2003). Twenty-First Century Health Promotion: The Public Health Revolution Meets the Wellness Revolution. *Health Promotion International, 18*(4), 275–278.

Nielsen, N. C., Murray, J., & Zysman, J. (2013). *The Services Dilemma: Productivity Sinkhole or Commoditization?* Verve Books. Retrieved September 10, 2017, from http://www.brie.berkeley.edu/wp-content/uploads/2016/03/Services-Dilemma.pdf

Pilzer, P. Z. (2007). *The New Wellness Revolution: How to Make a Fortune in the Next Trillion Dollar Industry?* (2nd ed.). Hoboken: John Wiley & Sons.

The Economist. (2007, January 4). *The Wellness Boom: Helping Consumers to Lead Healthy Lifestyles Is Becoming a Big Business*. Retrieved October 31, 2017, from http://www.economist.com/node/8492618

CHAPTER 2

The Conceptual Field of Wellness

Abstract This chapter starts with a conceptual clarification and the building of a conceptual model of wellness. The latter, referred to as the Y model of wellness, identifies eight dimensions, which serve as the basis for determining the major areas of wellness-oriented urban economic development. The conceptual investigation brings forth such concepts as basic human needs, well-being, quality of life, health, and welfare, which are all concepts as multi-dimensional and multi-layered as wellness. Among all these concepts, wellness has the closest connection with business, which is evident in its association with such industries as spa, beauty, fitness, meditation, and alternative medicine. The key challenge to local governments is to determine the best way of integrating the dimensions of wellness in their economic development, for each of them have unique preconditions and characteristics.

Keywords Wellness • Well-being • Welfare • Health • Human needs

As wellness is a vague concept, there is a good reason to start this journey with a conceptual clarification. This chapter introduces selected aspects of wellness discourse and the most important dimensions of the concept of wellness. Because of the fuzziness of this conceptual field, there is a need to take into account some other concepts, such as basic human needs,

A.-V. Anttiroiko, *Wellness City*,
https://doi.org/10.1007/978-3-319-75562-5_2

well-being, quality of life, health, and welfare, which are closely related to and often used interchangeably with the concept of wellness. As this discussion is devoted to generic concepts, "softer" and more specific terminology associated with wellness, including spa, fitness, beauty, relaxation, and stress reduction (see e.g. GSS 2010), is not elaborated in this section.

Conceptualizing Wellness

In the current discussion, wellness is associated with a positive lifestyle that contributes to people's healthiness. This point is well depicted by the Global Wellness Institute (2017, iii), which defined wellness as "the active pursuit of activities, choices, and lifestyles that lead to a state of holistic health." This view emphasizes the role of personal choice and individual responsibility for well-being through the practice of health-promoting lifestyle behavior. These practices can include such activities as self-actualization, health responsibility, exercise, nutrition, interpersonal support, and stress management, all supported by purposely designed environments, technologies, and methods (Walker et al. 1987). With respect to economy, this concept is primarily associated with spa, beauty, and fitness at its core and additionally with alternative medicine, meditation, spirituality, and a few other areas of, broadly understood, health-related human activity.

When we drill deeper into this concept, it seems less clear what wellness actually means and how it relates to human needs and, more than anything, how it relates to such concepts as well-being and health. There is thus a good reason to start the discussion about wellness-oriented economic development policy with the concept of wellness and its relationship with similar concepts. Another obvious need is to picture the conceptual scope of wellness, as such a clarification is vital for the understanding of its overall economic potential and of the synergistic relationships between its dimensions.

The framework of our conceptualization relies on four ontological categories (Hartmann 1953, 43–48; cf. Popper 1979): (1) animate beings; (2) consciousness; (3) spatial outer world; and (4) social entities. The first category comprises biological entities, including bodily existence, which is obviously at the core of wellness. The second realm, consciousness or broadly understood mental objects and events, includes two fundamental strata: psychic and spiritual. The last two categories represent two sides of the generic environment, physical and social, in which biological and mental processes are embedded, to which they react, and which they occasionally try to change. The physical side refers to inanimate things and physical structures and processes, while the social side refers to social institutions and structures, and to a range of social entities—such as scientific knowledge, myths, tools, and works of art with varying degrees of physical and socio-cultural embeddedness. These last two categories essentially form a constellation of both concrete and abstract objects of the world that cannot be reduced either to animate being or to human consciousness, or—as usually referred to in wellness discourse—to body and mind. We may call them the environment, or in a more abstract way the context, within which the existence of conscious human beings takes place.

Concerning bodily existence, we will expand the narrow lifestyle-related view of wellness to various health care activities. There are three particular reasons for this. First, there are many occasions where it is impossible to draw a meaningful line between these two concepts. Such an arbitrary demarcation is not useful, especially from the point of view of local economic development. Second, if we narrow our view of wellness to spa, beauty, fitness, and alternative medicine, it would be too limiting a view considering the huge potential relating to health care. This extension is done with knowing that one of the cornerstones of wellness discourse is a distinction between traditional health care or "illness care" associated with a medical paradigm and healthy lifestyle that pursues holistic health associated with a wellness paradigm. This takes us to our third point. It is likely that health care and wellness will increasingly merge in the near future, which urges us to consider them not only as supplementary but also as increasingly mutually reinforcing aspects of human well-being.

A broad understanding of the scope of wellness includes mental wellness, which is a basic category included in all wellness typologies. However, it is possible to include several other dimensions to this category for a comprehensive picture of mental well-being or a "mind continuum," including social, cultural, intellectual, and spiritual dimensions of wellness.

Another important dimension of wellness includes supporting structures, institutions, and devices, which is the third main category of the broad field of wellness. They have an essential role in the big picture of wellness, as nature, built environment, commercial amenities, and technological solutions are enablers of wellness-oriented activities. This refers to the socio-technical environment on which wellness is embedded in a modern societal setting.

The previously described building blocks of wellness domains and their subcategories are presented in Fig. 2.1. Due to the shape of the demarcation lines between the three main categories, it is called the *Y model of wellness*. The content of each category of this scheme is further elaborated in Chap. 5.

The idea behind the Y model of wellness is to emphasize the key aspects of wellness in terms of urban economic development. More than anything it stresses the need to take a view on wellness that goes beyond narrowly defined personal health. Another important factor is its emphasis on the multi-dimensionality of wellness and the interrelatedness of various domains of wellness. Having said that, it must be remembered that the root of the concept of wellness is ultimately in a holistic view of personal health, usually presented as a triad of body, mind, and soul (Dunn 1959). It emphasizes personal responsibility and related proactive orientation, lifestyle, and activities that achieve an optimal state of individual health and well-being (cf. Smith and Puczkó 2009; Dvorak et al. 2014; Global

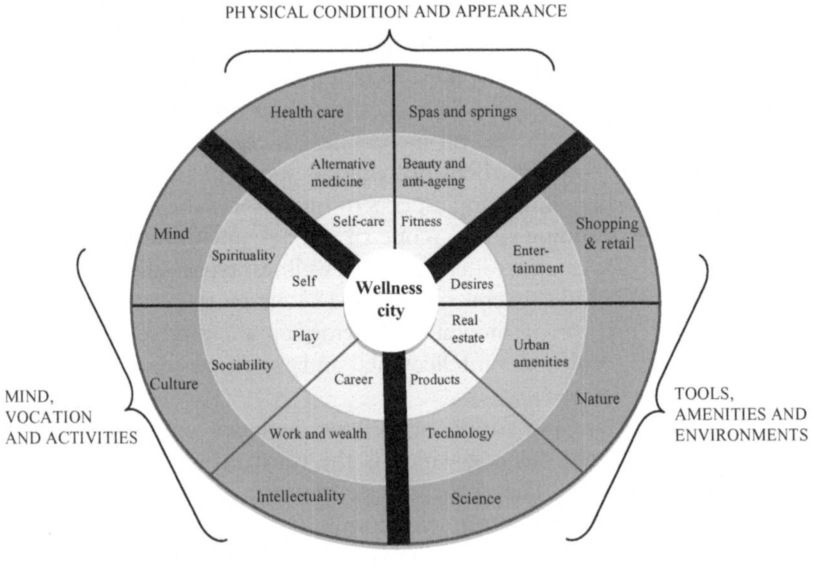

Fig. 2.1 The Y model of wellness

Wellness Institute 2015). This is the ultimate criterion for determining whether an entity is, in an essential sense, about wellness.

The price to pay for such a broad understanding of wellness is evidently a certain degree of loss of conceptual sharpness. The most obvious implication is that wellness as a development-oriented conception becomes an umbrella concept that is used to pinpoint a wide range of activities rooted in human well-being. This view is useful for local developers who need to capture the idea of wellness as a cluster that creates business opportunities, attracts investments, and provides jobs for both skilled and unskilled labor.

Basic Human Needs, Well-being, and Quality of Life

At a fundamental level, wellness has its root in the fulfillment of ***basic human needs***. The understanding of the latter was for a long time rather scattered field of study of various factors that affect human behavior and satisfaction, until Abraham Maslow (1943, 1954) synthesized the research on human motivation and presented his famous hierarchy of needs (Huitt 2007). His original conception included five levels of need: physiological; safety and security; belongingness and love; esteem; and self-actualization. This scheme assumes that lower level needs must be met before human motivation is directed to higher-level needs. Hence, the idea of a hierarchical nature of basic human needs.

Later Maslow (1987, 1999) identified two other categories, cognitive and aesthetic needs, as preceding self-actualization, and also added a particular form of self-actualization, or rather a level that transcends it, that of self-transcendence, which reflects a human need to connect with something spiritual or otherwise bigger than one's self (Maslow 1971). An appropriate way to interpret all these later amendments is to see them as subcategories, or nuances, of self-actualization included in the original five-level model (McGregor 2010). This is actually in line with Maslow's description of the four lowest level needs as ***deficiency needs***, while the further elaborated four higher level needs are ***actualization needs***, as depicted in Fig. 2.2.

There are plenty of theories that discuss human motivation and needs, including: Clayton P. Alderfer's Existence-Relatedness-Growth scheme (Alderfer 1972); Frederick Herzberg's two-factor theory of motivation (Herzberg et al. 1959; Herzberg 1966); David C. McClelland's human motivation theory, known as the three needs theory, referring to achievement, affiliation, and power (McClelland 1961); Manfred Max-Neef's

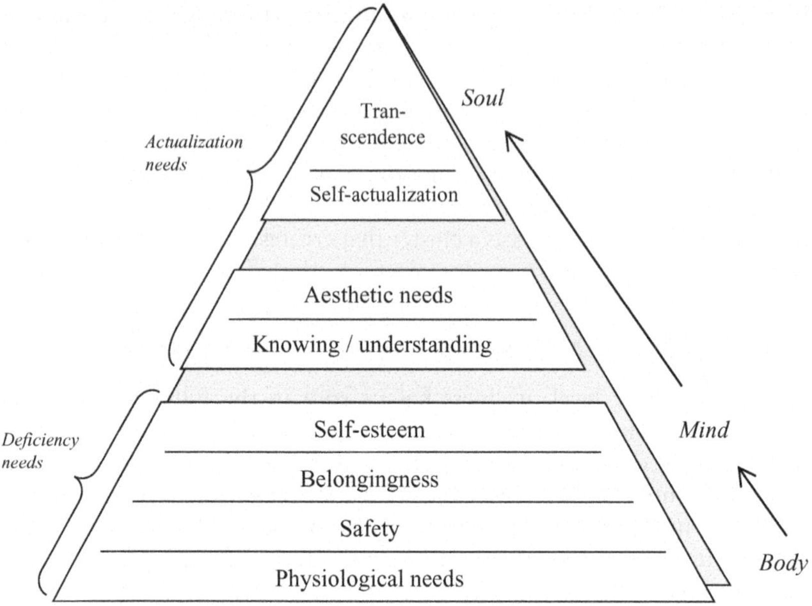

Fig. 2.2 Maslow's hierarchy of needs and three wellness categories. (Source: Modified from Huitt 2007)

(1991) taxonomy of fundamental human needs and related idea of human scale development; and so forth, each with their own strengths and weaknesses. The secret behind the wide acceptance of Maslow's theory among these is its intuitive appeal and clarity. It has similarities with some of the classic views in psychology and social philosophy, such as William James' (1890/1950, 1892/1962) division of an "empirical me" of the self into three categories: the material self, the social self, and the spiritual self (see also Mathes 1981).

No theory is without challenges, however, and Maslow's theorization is no exception. One critical question is whether our basic human needs actually form a hierarchy in the strict sense of the word; the other being the question of how universal or context-free these categories actually are. Many alternative theorizations, such as the one by Max-Neef (1991), identify wider sets of human needs and are arguably more nuanced and contextual than Maslow's, yet the latter seems to have surpassed them in simplicity and intuitive appeal.

Another generic category of particular importance in wellness discourse is *well-being*. Human well-being is an equally broad concept as basic human needs, even though the former is slightly more positive and prescriptive than the latter, which is rooted in a deep understanding of the human condition with a focus on the deprivation side of needs. Well-being is nevertheless an elusive concept with a diversity of dimensions, which creates a confusing base for research (Dodge et al. 2012). Concerning its core meaning, it can be understood as a subjective assessment of the current state of an individual, that is, how well a person's needs are met. Just like any of the basic terms associated with wellness, well-being is also multi-layered and multi-dimensional (McGillivray 2007). It can be subjective or objective, individual or collective (King 2007), and be about physical, economic, social, or psychological dimensions of well-being (McGregor 2010; McGillivray 2007).

Contextual conceptualizations of well-being contain several dimensions, as, for example, the eight quality of life domains identified in the Canadian Index of Wellbeing, including community vitality, democratic engagement, education, environment, healthy populations, leisure and culture, living standards, and time use (University of Waterloo n/a). Unfortunately, such a broad definition tends to increase terminological confusion. To keep the discussion focused, let us confine ourselves to overlaps and differences between the concepts of wellness and well-being. Wellness can be seen as a process that contributes to *physical, mental, and spiritual well-being*, which in turn is contended state of being *happy, healthy, and prosperous* (King 2007). This leads us to a demarcation proposed by Ellis (2017). She assumes that well-being was gradually set apart from wellness due to its association with measuring happiness and publicizing happiness indexes, such as Bhutan's Gross National Happiness Index developed in 2010, or the criteria used in the World Happiness Report, first published in 2012. Accordingly, the closer the relationship between well-being and happiness, the less it has to do with the essence of wellness, especially if the latter is understood as preventive actions intended to maintain or improve health. As appealing as it would be to usehappiness (i.e. a feeling of being happy) as a key to the demarcation between these to two central concepts, the concept of happiness represents insufficiently the essence of non-economic or non-material aspects of well-being. Another direction where we may seek the demarcation is that well-being is usually a more objective category than wellness, as for example in OECD's (2016) report "Well-being in Danish Cities."

Well-being is a generic concept, which gives it a special role in the conceptual field discussed in this book. It can be used to encompass the same or an even broader scope than lifestyle-oriented holistic wellness (McGregor 2010). What blurs the conceptual demarcation between well-being and wellness is the fact that occasionally wellness is used in as a generic way as well-being. In addition, the multi-dimensionality of both concepts leads to more or less similar descriptions of their key dimensions, even though the dimensions of well-being may seem to cover a broader scope than those of wellness. Rath and Harter (2010), for example, distinguish five universal, interconnected elements that shape our well-being, those of career, social, financial, physical, and community well-being, which is somewhat similar to the descriptions of the dimensions of wellness. Furthermore, contextual developments cause the same kind of blurring due to the use of well-being as a reflection of the change of subjectivity or, in a more concrete sense, due to a transition from subjects as citizens to subjects as consumers, the latter conceiving well-being as a normative obligation chosen and sought after by individual agents (Sointu 2005). This again makes it fairly similar to the concept of wellness.

Well-being has a conceptual connection with another widely used concept, *quality of life* (QOL) (King et al. 2014; Andrews and Withey 1976), not least because QOL has been defined as the general well-being of individuals. The following definition of well-being reveals this conceptual connection particularly well: well-being is an assessment of a person's quality of life according to his own chosen criteria (Shin and Johnson 1978). Well-being can broadly describe the aspects of wellness, while QOL is usually associated with an evaluative approach to well-being. In terms of content, QOL bears many similarities to the concept of well-being, for example, in having both subjective and objective sides and a similar set of dimensions. It seems though that QOL is conceptually becoming 'softer', describing the standard of health, comfort, and happiness experienced by an individual, as opposed to the level of subsistence, wealth, or material welfare, most commonly described by the concept *standard of living*.

To sum up, while there are family resemblances between basic human needs, well-being, quality of life, and wellness, they differ to a degree in terms of the context of their use. All these terms are fairly generic and multi-dimensional. We have approached them here from a rather subjectivist perspective, as it helps to maintain conceptual clarity and an inherent connection with wellness discourse. However, it is important to keep in mind that all these concepts allow both subjective and objective interpretations. They can also be applied to groups of people with varying sizes and degrees of social integration, including families, local communities, societies, and, in the broadest sense, the global population (cf. Prilleltensky and Prilleltensky 2012). It is noteworthy that in this comparison wellness is generally more process-oriented and subjectivist, and also more commonly used in business contexts, than any other previously discussed concept.

Health, Health Care, and Welfare

Health has always been at the core of wellness discourse, which makes these concepts closely related. Health is generally known as a person's mental or physical condition, or simply being free from illness. It has, just like most other wellness-related concepts, both subjective and objective sides and different layers, a major distinction being between the experienced health of an individual and an aggregated health of territorial communities. Even if it is not as broad as basic human needs, well-being, or quality of life, it is usually seen as multi-dimensional, as defined by the World Health Organization (WHO 2017): "Health is a state of complete physical, mental and social well-being and not merely the absence of disease or infirmity." Such a broad definition takes it closer to the concepts of well-being and wellness.

Taking care of people's health is referred to as *health care*. It is conventionally defined as the organized provision of medical treatment and care of the physically and mentally ill, provided by professional health care organizations (Oxford Dictionaries 2017). The term is often used to refer to the *health care system* of a community or a country. It is sometimes seen as categorically different to wellness, the latter emphasizing personal choices that affect one's well-being (McGregor 2010). There are, however, intersections in which it is meaningless or even impossible to distinguish between wellness and health care, which is obvious in such areas as public health or wellness services that involve medical treatment.

What is noteworthy is that health can be used as an umbrella concept in such areas as health tourism, which can then be divided into medically oriented (operations, cosmetic surgery, illness-related rehabilitation, etc.) or wellness oriented (beauty treatments, fitness, meditation, etc.) health tourism, supplemented by an intersection that includes both elements (therapeutic recreation, lifestyle-related rehabilitation, occupational wellness, etc.) (Smith and Puczkó 2009; see also Smith and Puczkó 2017).

There is also discussion about health and well-being destinations, which explicitly broadens discussion from a medical to a wellness paradigm (Dvorak et al. 2014). When discussion turns to wellness in the context of health issues or health care, a decisive demarcation takes place between medical and wellness paradigms, the former referring to reactive treatment and cure of illness by health care institutions, and the latter to proactive maintenance and improvement of personal health (Global Wellness Institute 2015).

In this context, we can also take up the concept of *welfare*, which may be understood broadly as the state of doing well, especially in respect to good fortune, happiness, well-being, or prosperity. This reflects the original meaning of this concept, which is close to well-being. However, in the developed country context its modern meaning is associated with welfare society systems (Williams 1976), referring to statutory procedures and social programs designed to promote the basic physical and material well-being of people in need (Oxford Dictionaries 2017). As defined by Greve (2008, 58), "[w]elfare is the highest possible access to economic resources, a high level of well-being, including happiness, of the citizens, a guaranteed minimum income to avoid living in poverty, and, finally, having the capabilities to ensure the individual a good life."

Welfare is increased via various public policy programs, such as education, health care, housing, and social security. *Social welfare* refers to well-being in society, thus going beyond personal well-being to availability of social and welfare services and to such societal factors as environment, crime, and drug abuse (see Greve 2008). We do not have to see either welfare, or previously mentioned basic human needs or well-being, as fully subjective categories, for both the prerequisites for human actions and their consequences go beyond such subjectivity. There is thus something essentially relational and contextual in the proper understanding of concepts such as welfare (cf. Doyal and Gough 1984).

The *Differentia Specifica* of Wellness

Wellness is a member of the family of concepts that help to conceptualize the contextuality, multi-dimensionality, and multi-layeredness of the satisfaction of human needs. As shown above, beside wellness, they are referred to as basic human needs, well-being, quality of life, welfare, and health, depending on the conceptual requirement of each context of use. They bear some essential similarities—such as subjective vs. objective and individual vs. community dualities—and the same kind of multi-dimensionality, yet they are used in different discourses to emphasize different aspects or nuances of the satisfaction of holistically understood human needs. In this conceptual family wellness is currently understood as a process-oriented concept rooted in personal choices of, and responsibility in, holistic health, practiced through dedicated health-promoting lifestyle behaviors. Wellness revolves around health that is understood holistically, the latter dimension usually conceptualized as well-being. This provides sufficient guidance to search for its conceptual essence, as sketched in Fig. 2.3.

When thinking about the previously discussed family of wellness-related concepts, wellness includes a distinct association with business and economic life. In the business context, attention is directed to those industries that enable consumers to incorporate various aspects of wellness into their daily lives, including beauty and anti-aging treatments, healthy eating, nutrition and weight loss, health-motivated travel, fitness and mind-body activities, personalized, complementary, and alternative medicine, spas and thermal springs, workplace wellness, and wellness communities (Global Wellness Institute 2017). The wellness industry includes high-

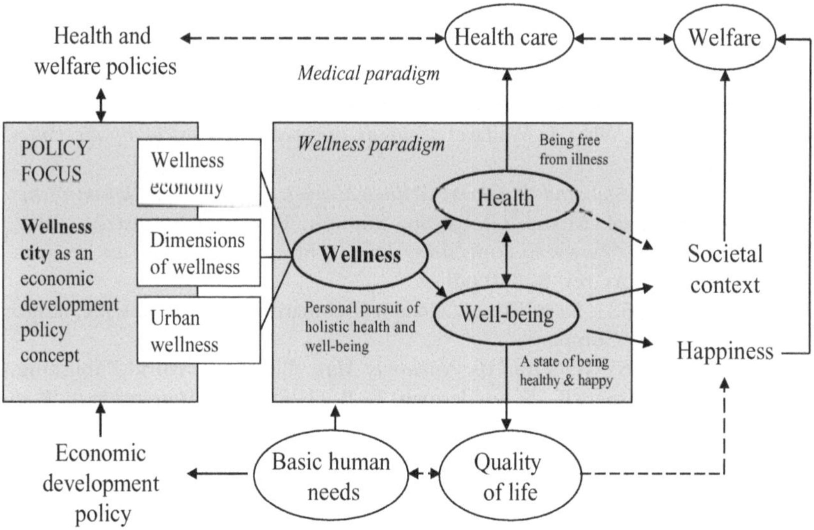

Fig. 2.3 Conceptual field of wellness city

value-adding activities, such as medicine in its entirety and wellness-related science and technology, which have direct or indirect connections with personal health and well-being.

References

Alderfer, C. (1972). *Existence, Relatedness, & Growth*. New York: Free Press.

Andrews, F. M., & Withey, S. B. (1976). *Social Indicators of Well-being: American's Perceptions of Life Quality*. New York: Plenum Press.

Dodge, R., Daly, A. P., Huyton, J., & Sanders, L. D. (2012). The Challenge of Defining Wellbeing. *International Journal of Wellbeing, 2*(3), 222–235.

Doyal, L., & Gough, I. (1984). A Theory of Human Needs. *Critical Social Policy, 4*(10), 6–38.

Dunn, H. L. (1959). High-Level Wellness for Man and Society. *American Journal of Public Health, 49*(6), 786–792.

Dvorak, D., Saari, S., & Tuominen, T. (Eds.). (2014). *Developing a Competitive Health and Well-being Destination*. Turku: Turku University of Applied Sciences.

Ellis, S. (2017). Wellness, Well-being … and What About Spa? *The Huffington Post*, April 13, 2016, Updated April 09, 2017. Retrieved September 17, 2017, from http://www.huffingtonpost.com/susie-ellis/wellness-wellbeingand-wha_b_9641722.html

Global Wellness Institute. (2015). *The Global Wellness Tourism Economy 2013 & 2014*. Miami: Global Wellness Institute.

Global Wellness Institute. (2017, January). *Global Wellness Economy Monitor*. Miami: Global Wellness Institute.

Greve, B. (2008). What Is Welfare? *Central European Journal of Public Policy, 2*(1), 50–73.

GSS. (2010, May). *Spas and the Global Wellness Market: Synergies and Opportunities*. SRI International. Miami: Global Spa Summit. Retrieved August 21, 2017, from https://www.sri.com/sites/default/files/publications/gss_sri_spasandwellnessreport_rev_82010.pdf

Hartmann, N. (1953). *New Ways of Ontology* (Reinhard C. Kuhn, trans.). Chicago: Henry Regnery Company.

Herzberg, F. (1966). *Work and the Nature of Man*. Cleveland: World Publishing.

Herzberg, F., Mausner, B., & Snyderman, B. B. (1959). *The Motivation to Work*. New York: John Wiley & Sons.

Huitt, W. (2007). *Maslow's Hierarchy of Needs. Educational Psychology Interactive*. Valdosta: Valdosta State University. Retrieved August 6, 2017, from http://www.edpsycinteractive.org/topics/conation/maslow.html

James, W. (1890/1950). *The Principles of Psychology* (Vol. 2). New York: Dover Publications.

James, W. (1892/1962). *Psychology: Briefer Course*. New York: Collier.

King, P. (2007, March). *The Concept of Wellbeing and Its Application in a Study of Ageing in Aotearoa New Zealand* (EWAS Working Paper 8). Retrieved August 10, 2017, from http://www.ewas.net.nz/Publications/filesEWAS/Conceptualising%20wellbeing.pdf

King, M. F., Renó, V. F., & Novo, E. M. L. M. (2014). The Concept, Dimensions and Methods of Assessment of Human Well-being Within a Socioecological Context: A Literature Review. *Social Indicators Research, 116*(3), 681–698.

Maslow, A. H. (1943). A Theory of Human Motivation. *Psychological Review, 50*, 370–396.

Maslow, A. H. (1954). *Motivation and Personality*. New York: Harper.

Maslow, A. H. (1971). *The Farther Reaches of Human Nature*. New York: The Viking Press.

Maslow, A. H. (1987). *Motivation and Personality* (3rd ed.). New York: Addison Wesley Longman.

Maslow, A. H. (1999). *Toward a Psychology of Being* (3rd ed.). New York: John Wiley & Sons.

Mathes, E. W. (1981). Maslow's Hierarchy of Needs as a Guide for Living. *Journal of Humanistic Psychology, 21*(4), 69–72.

Max-Neef, M. A. (1991). *Human Scale Development: Conception, Application, and Further Reflections*. New York/London: The Apex Press.

McClelland, D. C. (1961). *The Achieving Society*. Princeton: Van Nostrand Co.

McGillivray, M. (Ed.). (2007). *Human Well Being: Concept and Measurement*. Basingstoke: Palgrave Macmillan.

McGregor, S. L. T. (2010). *Well-being, Wellness and Basic Human Needs in Home Economics* (McGregor Monograph Series No. 201003). Seabright: McGregor Consulting Group. Retrieved August 1, 2017, from http://www.consultmcgregor.com/documents/publications/well-being_wellness_and_basic_human_needs_in_home_economics.pdf

OECD. (2016). *Well-being in Danish Cities*. Paris: OECD Publishing.

Oxford Dictionaries. (2017). *Dictionary* (Website). Oxford: Oxford University Press. Retrieved August 10, 2017, from https://en.oxforddictionaries.com/

Popper, K. R. (1979). *Objective Knowledge: An Evolutionary Approach* (Revised edition). Oxford: Oxford University Press.

Prilleltensky, I., & Prilleltensky, O. (2012). Webs of Well-being: The Interdependence of Personal, Relational, Organizational and Communal Well-being. In J. Haworth & G. Hart (Eds.), *Well-being: Individual, Community and Social Perspectives* (pp. 57–74). Basingstoke: Palgrave Macmillan.

Rath, T., & Harter, J. (2010). *Wellbeing: The Five Essential Elements*. New York: Gallup Press.

Shin, D. C., & Johnson, D. M. (1978). Avowed Happiness as an Overall Assessment of the Quality of Life. *Social Indicators Research, 5*(1–4), 475–492.

Smith, M., & Puczkó, L. (2009). *Health and Wellness Tourism* (2nd ed.). Oxford: Butterworth-Heinemann.

Smith, M. K., & Puczkó, L. (Eds.). (2017). *The Routledge Handbook of Health Tourism*. London/New York: Routledge.

Sointu, E. (2005). The Rise of an Ideal: Tracing Changing Discourses of Wellbeing. *The Sociological Review, 53*(2), 255–274.

University of Waterloo. (n/a). *Canadian Index of Wellbeing. Domains and Indicators*. Retrieved August 10, 2017, from https://uwaterloo.ca/canadian-index-wellbeing/what-we-do/domains-and-indicators

Walker, S. N., Sechrist, K. R., & Pender, N. J. (1987). The Health-Promoting Lifestyle Profile: Development and Psychometric Characteristics. *Nursing Research, 36*(2), 76–81.

WHO. (2017). *Constitution of WHO: Principles*. Geneva: World Health Organization. Retrieved August 10, 2017, from http://www.who.int/about/mission/en/

Williams, R. (1976). *Keywords: A Vocabulary of Culture and Society*. Glasgow: Fontana.

CHAPTER 3

Wellness and the City

Abstract Urban wellness draws attention to the relationship between holistic wellness and urban life. This chapter sheds light on the levels and dynamics of wellness in the city. It conceptualizes the city as a "dissipative structure" that integrates wellness resources and flows. Another topic discussed is an institutional view of wellness, with a focus on the governance field of local wellness economy. In the last two sections of the chapter, the concept of a wellness city is defined—first, as a generic urban phenomenon, and second, as a concept applied to the promotion of urban economic development.

Keywords Urban wellness • Dissipative structure • Governance • Wellness flows • Wellness economy

Wellness is not only a complex phenomenon but also has a multi-layered context and complicated connections with the ontological structures of the world. This book embeds the discussion about wellness in a particular life-world context, that of the urban. The reason for such a choice is that in respect of local economic development policy, our main references are larger urban communities in developed countries. In addition, it is worth remembering that even if remote resorts and wellness destinations have long been landmarks in the development of the spa industry, ongoing

A.-V. Anttiroiko, *Wellness City*,
https://doi.org/10.1007/978-3-319-75562-5_3

global transformations and, especially, emerging demand- and supply-side trends in health and wellness indicate the momentousness of urban wellness.

Wellness as a phenomenon has manifestations that reflect varying scales of the spatial organization of society. Its multi-layeredness is visible in its role in personal and family life, in wellness destinations, in neighborhoods, cities, regions, and societies as a whole. The core topic of this book—wellness-oriented urban economic development policy—is primarily a meso-level issue. A meso-level perspective on wellness can be either about dynamic processes and structures of subnational territorial communities or about institutionalized practices that concern those processes and structures that take place within organized environments. This chapter sheds light on the former, that is, urban wellness.

Wellness Flows and Urban Dissipative Structures

Cities are densely populated human settlements, which serve as the sites of social interaction that help to organize the collective action needed to take care of critical urban functions (see e.g. Kotkin 2005). In a simplified sense, these functions emerge in the interplay of production and consumption. To be more precise, we can identify four key functions that are vital for the functioning and development of the urban economy: investment, production, distribution, and consumption. Figure 3.1 illustrates the dynamic setting of wellness flows.

Even if local communities have been genuinely local throughout human history, they have always interacted with their broader context in one way or another. This is particularly true with larger cities, which have served as the loci of commerce, security, and power. Modernization has always included a tendency to delocalize, which brought deep changes to cities by tying them tightly to the politics and policies of nation-states and the establishment of modern institutions of governance.

The development of international relations and trade had a tremendous impact on cities, increasing their role as hubs of production, logistics, and trade. A major turn took place in this respect in the nineteenth century, sometimes referred to as the first wave of globalization, that after the hindrances of the interwar decades started to accelerate at an unprecedented pace and pave the way to a global age. This development had many drivers, some of the most obvious being global stability and security, decreased transportation and communication costs, and the liberalization of world trade (Ortiz-Ospina and Roser 2017).

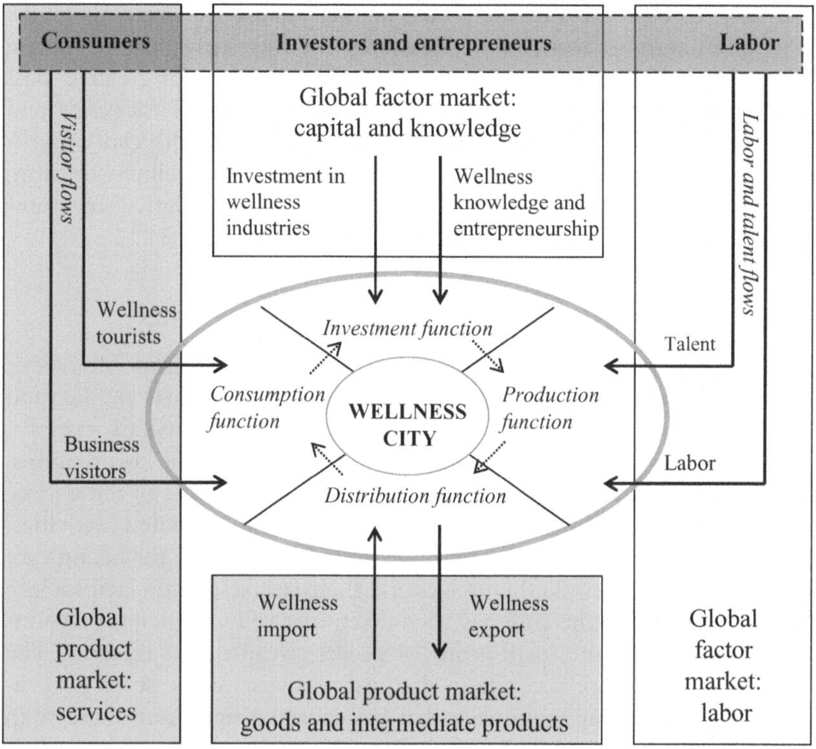

Fig. 3.1 City as an integrator of wellness flows. (Source: Applied from Anttiroiko 2015)

The intensification of world trade caused internal and relational changes in urban life. One way of understanding the nature of urban communities in an increasingly open and fluid global economy is to conceptualize them as ***dissipative structures*** (cf. Prigogine and Stengers 1984; Pulselli et al. 2005). Such an approach conceptualizes cities as innumerable flows of energy, matter, actions, and symbols. This implies that rather than perceiving cities as fixed places, we should view them essentially as hubs of flows and nodes of interaction (Anttiroiko 2015).

In the wellness economy, value flows take many shapes. Money flows globally when investors invest in wellness businesses with the expectation of financial return; knowledge on wellness is disseminated globally by universities, research institutes, corporate R&D units, and the media; and health products and equipment are exported from producers to retailers and then to customers in the global market. There are also immigrants who often start to work in wellness areas in their new host countries; experts and professionals who cross borders as a part of creative class migration; business visitors who attend wellness-related meetings and conventions; and tourists who cross borders to obtain health care or wellness services. A genuine manifestation of urban flows is wellness tourism, as it shows in a concrete way the dialectic of urban dissipative structures and their connection with material living (see Cooper 2015).

Governing Urban Wellness Development

Wellness has various manifestations in different subsystems of society, which are usually divided into three categories: voluntary, public, and business sectors. The first is associated with citizens and their associations, the second with government, and the last with for-profit corporations. There is no clearly identified pattern to determine the roles of these three realms of society in the development of wellness-related activities. However, we can roughly say that the main responsibility for taking care of wellness lies in people themselves and their families within civil society. Since ancient times the cure has been taken care of by trained professionals, supported by the institutions of power, wealth, and religion. The emergence of welfare societies in the post-war years witnessed a government intervention in health care that has caused a significant increase in public expenditure on health. The role of the business sector in providing health products, technological solutions, facilities, and services to meet the needs of diverse groups of wellness-minded consumers has increased its importance in the last few decades. In all, it is plausible to say that wellness has always been a more or less public-private-people mix with context-dependent variations in the weight of each sector.

Concerning local public governance of wellness-oriented local economic development, the key organization in Western democracies is *local government*, which bears responsibility in local public affairs, including infrastructure, welfare, and economic development. Concerning the latter, the main responsibility is with larger local governments vested to *development organizations*, such as development corporations, economic development agencies, convention and visitors bureaus, tourism boards, and destination management organizations (DMOs). As a wellness-oriented promotion of economic development relies essentially on privately organized destinations and private service providers, travel agencies, intermediary organizations, and a host of other stakeholders, local public organizations must integrate local efforts via partnerships and networks, and also represent their interests upwards and facilitate business and knowledge processes via national, macro-regional, and global networks (see Fig. 3.2). A traditional role of institutions of public governance in this field has been to take care of regulation

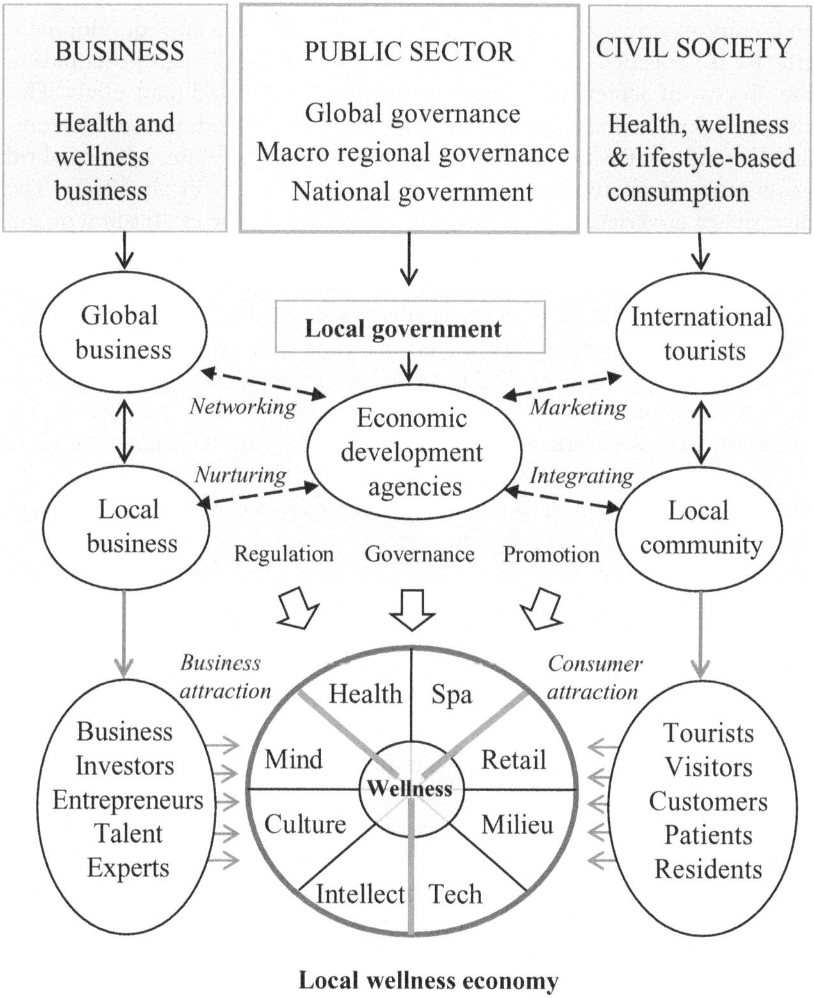

Fig. 3.2 The governance field of a local wellness economy

and to provide services, while recently network governance and promotional and development-oriented functions have become prominent.

The political core of local governance in representative democracy relies on hierarchical order. It is a de facto basis of the functioning of democratic institutions and public administration. However, since the late 1980s or early 1990s an ideological shift has changed the emphasis of the authority of government gradually into *governance* that has a persuasive, engaging, and empowering approach to public policy-making and development efforts. It is needed in the utilization of local resources and potentials in the process of achieving democratically decided development goals. This also applies to wellness promotion, which has both top-down and bottom-up elements, but which in practice relies on a mixed approach or hybrid governance (Christensen and Lægreid 2011; Skelcher et al. 2013). The diversity of governance models has its expression in the establishment and operations of DMOs, as they can be run by public authorities, corporations, non-profit organizations, or collaboratively (Dvorak et al. 2014).

As a whole, wellness as an internally diverse cluster sets special requirements on its promotion and related planning and governance activities. More often than not individual locations are highly dependent on particular natural resources, historical sites, expert institutions, or large-scale destinations, which requires that special attention is paid to partnerships and stakeholder relationship management. Partly for the same reason, any wellness-oriented cluster policy is inherently related to the management and development of major destinations in the locality (Dvorak et al. 2014).

Wellness City as an Urban Phenomenon

When we combine discussions about the concept of holistic wellness, the urban setting, and the pursuit of local economic development, their intersection can be referred to as a *wellness city*. It belongs to the family of such development-oriented concepts as industrial city, high-tech city, creative city, hub city, tourist city, and the like.

As shown in Chap. 2, wellness is a process-oriented concept rooted in an individual's pursuit of a health-promoting lifestyle that aims at holistic health and well-being. The urban dimension here is the context of densely populated human settlements, with infrastructures, technologies, and services that facilitate urban living. This leads to the following generic definition of a wellness city.

> As an urban phenomenon, *wellness city* refers to the structures and processes of an urban community, which in an integrated manner facilitates city dwellers' and visitors' pursuit of practicing a health-promoting lifestyle that aims at their holistic health and well-being.

Such a city forms an integrative and enabling urban structure in the sense that through mutually reinforcing policies, institutions, and actions of public, private, and voluntary organizations it is able to support various aspects of the holistic health and well-being of its residents and visitors.

The dimensions of wellness have a connection to various city formations and destinations, which are associated with some particular aspects of urban development. Let us map out these connections on the basis of a scheme derived from the previously mentioned Y model of wellness. A city conception that takes the bodily aspect of wellness as a starting point is, for example, a *health care city*, which obviously refers to a narrower phenomenon than that of a wellness city. Such a formation may be a special zone, district, or a new town project within a wider urban setting, such as Dubai Healthcare City in United Arab Emirates. An expression of the same trend, though in the form of an international city network, is the Healthy Cities movement, which aims to raise awareness of the role of place in achieving and maintaining health. Actions within this movement have usually been aimed at reducing crime and environmental degradation, increasing recreational spaces, and promoting connectedness between people on health, education, and quality of life. This movement includes thousands of cities worldwide, sharing a common aim of using intersectoral collaboration and community participation to respond to the compromises to health that flow from people's everyday lives, to promote a holistic view of health, and to inform policy. As an ideal, a Healthy City is "one where people have choices that allow them to reach their maximum potential" (McMurray and Clendon 2015, 30).

There are urban developments based on quality of life and lifestyle-oriented initiatives. Illuminating examples are towns, cities, and counties involved in the *Cittaslow* or Slow city movement (http://www.cittaslow.org/). The spiritual dimension of wellness is highlighted in such urban formations as *holy cities*, be it Vatican City inside the city of Rome in Italy, Jerusalem in Israel, Mecca in Saudi Arabia, or Varanasi in India. There are also special *pilgrim cities*, such as Mina, a neighboring city to Mecca in Saudi Arabia, which provides temporary accommodation for millions of pilgrims during the annual Hajj pilgrimage.

Many cities manifest either generic or specific aspects of wellness in their brand or economic profile, as for example Quezon City in Philippines, which describes itself as a *lifestyle city*. Furthermore, there are genuine *wellness communities* and new town projects, which are built with wellness as one of their guiding principles, including such widely discussed cases as Serenbe in Georgia and Lake Nona in Florida, and as a slightly different kind of creation, Dubai Lifestyle City, which is a gated community for wealthy people in the Dubailand area of Dubai, United Arab Emirates.

There is a range of cities of various sizes, city districts, and destinations that provide facilities and services on a commercial basis for body care, fitness, exercise, and consumption, including *spa towns* (e.g. Bath in the UK), *sports cities* and other urban outdoors facilities (e.g. Sportcity in Manchester, UK; Jaypee Sports City in India; and Dubai Sports City in Dubai, UAE), and *consumer and shopping cities* from New York to Hong Kong and Dubai with a wide range of world-class wellness salons, boutiques, and services.

Wellness city has a connection to a range of city conceptions that relate to urban living environments, infrastructures, and technologies, such as: *livable city* (e.g. Melbourne, Vienna, and Toronto); *sustainable city* (e.g. Portland, OR, Singapore, and Copenhagen); and *e-city*, *digital city*, or *smart city* (e.g. Barcelona, San Francisco, Seoul, and Helsinki). There are also such urban formations as *university city*, *college town*, *knowledge city*, *cultural city*, and *creative city* (e.g. Oxford, Salzburg, Kanazawa, and Palo Alto), which bring cultural experiences, learning, and creativity into the picture. All such city profiles have a connection with some dimension of the wellness city.

These connections not only help to position the wellness city in the field of urban development, but also to point out critical conceptual demarcations, which are needed to keep the concept of the wellness city rich, clear, and sufficiently concise. There are two guiding rules to bear in mind in this respect. First, the core idea of a holistic view of personal health helps to draw the line between a wellness city and other city-level policy concepts. Second, in some areas there is a natural conceptual overlap, as in the case of all-encompassing concepts like innovativeness, smartness, and sustainability, which penetrate to practically all aspects of urban development and have many linkages with urban wellness.

Let us take some examples. Knowledge city is a broad concept that includes the role of higher education institutions in local development, the infrastructure and channels of urban informatics, and so forth (see e.g.

Carrillo et al. 2014). It has, however, intersections with a wellness city in those areas that relate to health informatics and other wellness-related knowledge processes, intellectuality, and personal growth. Thus, promoting knowledge-based urban development in Melbourne or Boston is not a wellness project as such (e.g. Yigitcanlar et al. 2012), but when Osaka city promotes its development as a knowledge-intensive lifestyle city, it can be understood as part of broadly defined wellness city movement. In the same way, the concept of smart wellness city is a fusion of two trends in urban development, those of smartness and wellness, which was used to promote urban development in Niigata, Toyooka, and some other Japanese cities (Smith 2013). In the same vain, sustainable city is combined with wellness in such communities as the Grow Community near Seattle, which targets the health and happiness of inhabitants in the context of a sustainability action plan based on the ten One Planet Living principles (http://www.bioregional.com/grow-community/).

Wellness City in Economic Development Policy

As our focus is on local economic development, we can take a step away from the previous discussion to better comprehend our core concept. This requires us to pay attention to the promotion of wellness industries and the overall support to economic value creation within broadly defined local wellness cluster. Wellness industries at the core of the cluster create economic value and employment and business opportunities by serving customers who reactively want to improve their health or who proactively seek a lifestyle that contributes to their pursuit of an optimal state of well-being (cf. Global Wellness Institute 2017). The role of local government is decisive in the promotion of local economic development, as it articulates and aggregates local interests, designs and integrates local public policies, creates partnerships, and co-ordinates policy implementation. Taking these factors into account, a wellness city can be defined as a local economic development concept as follows.

> In the context of local economic development, *wellness city* is an economic policy concept that focuses on strategic development, policy-making, and public governance that through the promotion of wellness industries and related economic activities improves conditions for local economic growth, business opportunity enhancement, and community value generation.

In the context of economic development policy "wellness" and "city" intersect in areas that are dedicated to: wellness as innovation and export promotion environments; attractive wellness destinations for tourists; or wellness neighborhoods developed to meet the demand for wellness lifestyle environments and real estate. Wellness has traditionally been an attraction business. Thus, the most well-known formations of consciously built wellness cities are large-scale wellness destinations, resorts, and retreats, which are probably more numerous in rural or suburban areas than in inner cities. Many of them are within close proximity to cities, however, such as Mines Wellness City near Kuala Lumpur, which is a primary example of a large-scale, integrated health and wellness resort. This scene is changing quickly though, for a new generation of health care hubs, wellness communities, and lifestyle cities is rising as corporate, government, or partnership-based regeneration and new town projects emerge to attract investment and create new businesses and jobs. Urban wellness has started to draw local developers' attention for two reasons: its significance to seeking everyday well-being in urban communities; and its obvious potential to facilitate local economic development and contribute to local prosperity.

References

Anttiroiko, A.-V. (2015). *New Urban Management: Attracting Value Flows to Branded Hubs*. Basingstoke: Palgrave Macmillan.

Carrillo, F. J., Yigitcanlar, T., García, B., & Lönnqvist, A. (2014). *Knowledge and the City: Concepts, Applications and Trends of Knowledge-Based Urban Development*. New York/London: Routledge.

Christensen, T., & Lægreid, P. (2011). Complexity and Hybrid Public Administration—Theoretical and Empirical Challenges. *Public Organization Review, 11*(4), 407–423.

Cooper, M. (Ed.). (2015). *Current Issues and Emerging Trends in Medical Tourism*. Hershey: IGI Global.

Dvorak, D., Saari, S., & Tuominen, T. (Eds.). (2014). *Developing a Competitive Health and Well-being Destination*. Turku: Turku University of Applied Sciences.

Global Wellness Institute. (2017, January). *Global Wellness Economy Monitor*. Miami: Global Wellness Institute.

Kotkin, J. (2005). *The City: A Global History*. London: Weidenfeld and Nicolson.

McMurray, A., & Clendon, J. (2015). *Community Health and Wellness: Primary Health Care in Practice* (5th ed.). Chatswood: Elsevier.

Ortiz-Ospina, E., & Roser, M. (2017). *International Trade. Our World in Data* (Online Publication). Retrieved August 14, 2017, from https://ourworldindata.org/international-trade

Prigogine, I., & Stengers, I. (1984). *Order Out of Chaos: Man's New Dialogue with Nature*. London: Heinemann.

Pulselli, R. M., Pulselli, F. M., Ratti, C., & Tiezzi, E. (2005, September 11–14). Dissipative Structures for Understanding Cities: Resource Flows and Mobility Patterns. In A. Halim Boussabaine, J. Lewis, R. J. Kirkham, & G. E. M. Jared (Eds.), *Proceeding of the 1st International Conference on Built Environment Complexity*. Becon: University of Liverpool. Retrieved August 17, 2017, from https://pdfs.semanticscholar.org/5486/97ddb03bda99c0539114fe13dbfb1cb4c4fe.pdf

Skelcher, C., Sullivan, H., & Jeffares, S. (2013). *Hybrid Governance in European Cities: Neighborhood, Migration and Democracy*. Basingstoke: Palgrave Macmillan.

Smith, R. D. (2013, August). Regional Cities Revitalize: Smart Wellness City, machi-zukuri. Highlighting Japan. *Feature: Livable Cities*, pp. 6–11. Retrieved August 17, 2017, from http://dwl.gov-online.go.jp/video/cao/dl/public_html/gov/pdf/hlj/20130801/06-11.pdf

Yigitcanlar, T., Metaxiotis, K., & Carillo, F. J. (2012). *Building Prosperous Knowledge Cities: Policies, Plans and Metrics*. Cheltenham: Edward Elgar.

CHAPTER 4

Wellness in Local Economic Development

Abstract This chapter explores the core topic of this book, the role of wellness in urban economic development. Discussion starts with a brief description of the major trends behind the wellness revolution and continues with a brief introduction to the wellness economy. From the characterization of the wellness economy, the discussion moves to local policy making, followed by a brief outline of local asset analysis, which helps to determine the initial local conditions for wellness-oriented economic development. The last section of the chapter provides an outline of the preconditions for wellness-oriented cluster policy.

Keywords Wellness trends • Wellness industries • Asset analysis • Wellness cluster • Cluster policy

Having mapped out the conceptual field of wellness and its connection with urban development in previous chapters, it is time to look at the third element that determines our approach to a wellness city: the economy. Economy describes the aggregate value generation processes directed to the use of scarce resources through investment, production, distribution, and consumption functions, and the related aggregate economic outcomes within a territorial community. Strategic local economic development is the art of carefully interpreting signals of economic trends and of responding to them swiftly and wisely for the purpose of promoting local

A.-V. Anttiroiko, *Wellness City*,
https://doi.org/10.1007/978-3-319-75562-5_4

prosperity. Signs of the increased importance of wellness in economic life saw the light of day in the 1990s and more so in the 2000s. One of the prophets of this shift was Paul Pilzer (2007) with his idea of the rise of wellness as "the next trillion dollar industry." He compared this change with the revolutionary impacts of automobiles, airline travel, personal computers, and family planning, each of which provided huge business opportunities for those who pioneered their utilization. The next big thing of the twenty-first century—or at least one of them—is, according to Pilzer, the wellness revolution.

Factors Behind the Surge in a Wellness Economy

Challenges to local economic development in the global age are manifold. They include the latest phase of globalization, the rise of a digital economy, financial crises, demographic changes, income polarization, climate change, and a host of other trends (Leigh and Blakely 2013; see also Blair and Carroll 2009). While these all affect urban wellness in one way or another, the positive growth prospects of a wellness economy are the result of a large global middle class, the aging of post-industrial societies, emerging consumer trends, new cutting-edge wellness technologies, and a continuously evolving collective awareness of the preconditions for a good life and holistic well-being (see e.g. Ancarani and Gisco 2014). This development has factually long roots affected by post-industrialism, welfare society development, and rising salary levels, and includes a range of post-modern trends and reactions to the conditions of modern life.

Regarding the critical background factor of this development, the key social process is modernization that evolved in parallel with industrialization, starting in Europe in the eighteenth century. According to Anthony Giddens (1992), *modernity* is a result of an interplay of a few profound trends, those of capitalism, industrialism, surveillance and information control of the nation-state, and the development of military power. Features that characterize *modernization* include the accelerated pace of change, time–space separation (including the standardization of time and expansion of space through technological advancements), disembedding mechanisms that operate through symbolic tokens and expert systems, the emergence of hierarchical institutions that reflect general tendencies of social fragmentation and increased division of labor, and increased reflexivity at both personal and institutional levels (Giddens 1992). Manifestations of this development can be seen in such areas of modern life as paid labor, mass-consumption, division of labor in the economy, political institutions of the nation-state, and the enlightenment, and the idea of progress as a kind of grand narrative of modernity. What makes the development of the structures and institutions of modernity significant for wellness is the emergence of *public health* as an important policy issue, *health care* as an institutionalized professional system, and the *welfare society* as an all-encompassing social structure designed to guarantee universal services and thus a healthy life for all members of society. All these factors have contributed to the making of the modern "illness care" machinery.

Theorizations of late modernity, or *post-modernity*, is based on the identification and analysis of disjunctures in modern life—empirically starting around the 1960s and accelerating since the 1990s or so—which implies that the major features of a modern society have been radicalized, fragmented, or dissolved (Giddens 1992). We can see this in the fragmented working life, new forms of personalized and responsible consumption, the globalization of finance and other sectors of the economy, crumbling hierarchies of modern nation-states, the rise of feminism, environmentalism, and global social movements, and the fragmentation of values in society (see e.g. Castells 1997). The idea of post-modernity refers to an age of relativism, fragmentation, and pluralism, as popularized by Jean-François Lyotard (1984). In the context of wellness, the post-modern turn reflects our challenges in coping with an accelerating pace of change, as eloquently described by Alvin Toffler decades ago in his seminal book *Future Shock* (1970), and in the emergence of a post-materialism that emphasizes self-expression and quality of life over economic success, as described in Ronald Inglehart's influential *The Silent Revolution* (1977). These developments have inherent connections with the rise of new ideas and visions of holistically understood healthy living, which gave inspiration to wellness discourse and fueled wellness tourism, lifestyle real estate, the use of wellness wearables, and several other areas of the wellness economy (see Hueltenschmidt et al. 2013).

The previous discussion hints that demand side changes are rooted in the behavior of a well-off *middle class*. They have money but they are also stressed and at times overwhelmed by the burdens of a modern lifestyle, and thus seek not only short breaks or refreshing holidays but more durable solutions for living healthy, happy, and full lives. At the same time, younger generations, while not as affluent as the gray generation, are more inclined to "downshift" and seek alternative lifestyles that emphasize sharing, sustainability, and social responsibility, and at one end of this lifestyle, a free and easy-going life of the Go-Nowhere Generation or the Generation Why Bother, for which welfare dependency is a way of life (Green Carmichael 2012). In all, these and various other social trends—virtual identities, fragmentation of families, mainstreaming LGBT, and new social divisions—together with opportunities provided by technological advancements have attracted the attention of the corporate world, urged a new role for actors in civil society, and posed challenges to governments in promoting public health, which as a whole have made wellness one of the megatrends of our time (Dvorak et al. 2014).

To concretize this issue, the Global Wellness Institute (GWI) (2017) identifies three major trends—wealth, needs, and awareness—behind the growth of wellness economy:

- Wealthy middle class demand health products and devices, co-produce health and wellness services, and participate in activities that improve their health, well-being, and quality of life, which is visible in wellness travel, digital media, and higher education.
- There is increasing interest among consumers in all things related to maintaining and improving health, driven by aging, rising global epidemic of chronic disease and stress, the health problems caused by environmental degradation, supplemented by the view that "illness care" and the medicalism of modern health care system fails to improve the quality of life.
- Educated and affluent segments of the population are increasingly aware that their choices convey meaning, purpose, and impact beyond their own personal gratification. Consumers seek experiences that are anchored in authenticity, localness, uniqueness, and nature, and connects them with the well-being of other people and in its widest sense that of the whole planet.

The GWI (2017) reminds us that there are also risks, challenges, and hindrances that have had a significant impact on the trajectory of wellness, including rising income inequality, lack of evidence-based knowledge on the health benefits of wellness products, services and modalities, and controversial issues in politics and policies of wellness, such as the debate over wellness-related incentives and sanctions.

Wellness Economy

Let us next discuss the significance and composition of the wellness economy. This matter is sensitive to the kind of territorial community we talk about, for there are huge variations in the role of wellness sectors between localities. In some spa and resort towns, jobs may depend significantly on a narrowly defined wellness industry, while in some larger industrialized cities its share can be fairly modest. In any case, there are indications of the increase in the overall impact of wellness on the economy, as evidenced by various global trends (GWI 2017). Let us start with a brief look at the composition and size of the global wellness economy.

A key institution in making sense of the global wellness economy is the aforementioned GWI, a non-profit organization that has become a leading global research and educational resource for the core wellness industries (www.globalwellnessinstitute.org). Before measuring the size of this sector or cluster, we should know what industries are included in the wellness economy. The GWI (2017, iii) defines the wellness economy loosely as encompassing industries that enable consumers to incorporate wellness activities and lifestyles into their daily lives. The GWI has done invaluable work in defining the composition of the wellness economy and estimating its size based on various statistical sources, surveys, interviews, and literature. The first report of this kind was the 2014 "Global Spa and Wellness Economy Monitor." The later edition of the monitor, using data from 2015, estimates that the global wellness economy reached the level of USD 3.7 trillion, having grown at a faster pace than the global economy as a whole and representing more than 5% of global economic output (GWI 2017). That figure includes the following ten sectors (global expenditure in 2015 in brackets):

- Beauty and anti-aging (USD 999 billion): beauty and salon services (excluding spas), skin, hair and nail care products and services, cosmetics, toiletries and other personal care products; dermatology; prescription pharmaceuticals for skin care; products and services that specifically address age-related health and appearance issues, such as cosmetics and cosmeceuticals for skin, face and body care, hair care and growth, and pharmaceuticals and supplements that treat age-related health conditions.
- Healthy eating, nutrition, and weight loss (USD 648 billion): vitamins and supplements, herbal and traditional products, fortified and

functional foods and nutraceuticals, natural and organic foods, sports nutrition, and weight loss or weight management products and services.

- Wellness tourism (USD 563 billion): the aggregation of all expenditures made by wellness tourists, including primary, secondary, domestic, and international, comprising spending on lodging, food and beverage, activities and excursions, shopping, and in-country transportation.
- Fitness and mind-body (USD 542 billion): gyms and health clubs; personal training; yoga, Pilates, Tai Chi, martial arts and other mind-body practices; fitness and exercise clothing; fitness and exercise equipment and devices.
- Preventive and personalized medicine and public health (USD 534 billion): medical services that focus on treating healthy people, preventing disease, or detecting risk factors (routine exams, screening tests, etc.). Note: personalized health creates and uses sophisticated data for individual patients—genetic screening and diagnostics, personalized disease management, health records, and so on—to provide tailored approaches for preventing disease, diagnosing and managing risk factors, or managing and treating conditions.
- Complementary and alternative medicine (USD 199 billion): diverse medical, health care, or holistic systems, practices, and products that are not generally considered to be part of conventional medicine or the dominant health care system, including homeopathic, naturopathic, chiropractic, traditional Chinese medicine, Ayurveda, energy healing, meditation, herbal remedies, etc.
- Wellness lifestyle real estate (USD 119 billion): the market of residential, hospitality, and mixed-used real estate that incorporates the elements of human, social, and environmental health into its design, construction, amenities, services, and programming.
- Spa industry (USD 99 billion): spas and the related cluster of sectors that support and enable spa businesses, including such components as spa facilities, spa education, spa consulting, spa capital investments, spa association, and spa-related media and events.
- Thermal and mineral springs (USD 51 billion): the revenue-earning business establishments associated with the wellness, recreational, and therapeutic uses of water with special properties, including thermal water, mineral water, and seawater.

- Workplace or occupational wellness (USD 43 billion): expenditure on programs, services, activities, and equipment by employers aimed at improving their employees' health and wellness. These measures aim to raise awareness, provide education, and offer incentives that address specific health risk factors and behaviors (e.g. lack of exercise, poor eating habits, stress, or smoking) and encourage employees to adopt healthier lifestyles.

The relative weight and estimated worth of the global wellness economy and its connections with closely related industries are illustrated in Fig. 4.1 (numbers in the figure are only indicative of global market values).

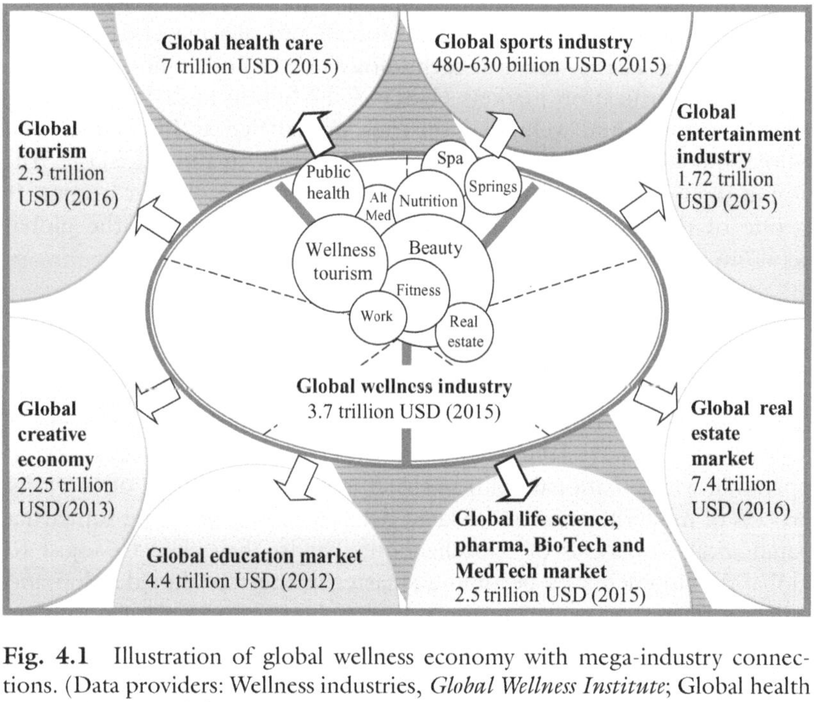

Fig. 4.1 Illustration of global wellness economy with mega-industry connections. (Data providers: Wellness industries, *Global Wellness Institute*; Global health care, *Deloitte*; Global sports industry, *A.T. Kearney*; Global entertainment industry, *PwC/Statista*; Global real estate market, *MSCI*; Global life science etc., *Deloitte*; Global education market, *Sean Cavanagh/EdWeek*; Global creative economy, *Richard Florida/CityLab*; Global tourism, *Statista*)

While the core wellness industry was estimated to be around USD 3.7 trillion in the mid-2010s, it is surrounded by a group of wellness-related high value-added industries, including health care (global market size estimated to be around USD 7 trillion in 2015), which we call, combined, *Wellness+*. As the statistics show, the health care sector is huge by volume. It produces goods and services to treat patients with preventive, curative, rehabilitative, and palliative care. People are usually familiar with hospitals and health care centers, but the system as a whole forms a complex professional field with many medical specialties. As a broad set of human health activities, in industrial classification systems health care includes such areas as hospital activities, medical and dental practice activities, and other human health activities (see e.g. McMurray and Clendon 2015).

Health care industry also includes such high-value-adding industries as health care equipment, pharmaceuticals, and a range of areas of life sciences. In this book, life sciences, biotech and pharmaceuticals (USD 2.1 trillion in 2015), medical technology (USD 369 billion in 2015), and medical education markets (USD 27.17 billion in 2016), together with health care and wellness industries, are labeled as *Wellness++*. As a whole, the *Wellness++* as a global economy was worth about USD 13 trillion in the mid-2010s, making about 18% of global economic output. It is one of the largest industries, if not the largest one, in the global economy.

Wellness on the Local Economic Development Agenda

One of the social ontological bases for local economic development is local choice (Stewart 1983). Subnational territorial communities, even if operating within national political structures and boundaries, after a long process of modernization and related delocalization, are facing somewhat paradoxical tendencies of relocalization, that is, they need to adjust to global developments by becoming smarter in the way they develop and utilize local resources and in the way they interact with their economic environment. During the past few centuries organized capitalism was conditioned by a firm national framework that, due to a new "permissive" global order, has been paving the way to an age of uncertainty (Lash and Urry 2007), which evidently calls for smart locally designed responses (Leigh and Blakely 2013; Kresl and Fry 2005).

Local economic development is a special function of *local government* that has a long history. Its relevance increased in the post-war years in the developed world and became more pronounced in the middle of the 1980s as a result of the conjunction of particular economic developments, most notably a crisis in traditional industries, the widespread emergence of high-tech sectors, and the gradual expansion of the services economy. There were also accompanying social trends that increased the need for balanced and proactive local actions, from persistent unemployment to social exclusion and urban unrest, coupled with political factors that profoundly changed the environment of many localities, such as decentralization reforms, the crisis of the welfare state, and economic integration within macro-regions, the most advanced among them being the European Union (Jouen et al. 2010).

Local economic development refers to the process through which relevant local actors and institutions mobilize themselves to initiate, reinforce, or entrench activities that strive for collectively decided economic goals using local resources added to those it has been able to attract to the area. It is a bottom-up process put forth by local actors to improve incomes, employment opportunities, and quality of life. It is needed as a response to the failure of markets and national government policies that prefer local solutions to development challenges (cf. OECD 2001).

When considering the relevance of different industries or sectors of the wellness economy we can apply some guidelines of conventional *cluster policy* (e.g. Economics Center for Education and Research 2004; OECD 2010; European Commission 2013). While promoting selected areas of local economy, local governments pay attention to local uniqueness, location specificity, local assets, and relational capital, which tie activities to a particular locality, as in the cases of hot springs or beaches, which in a very concrete way reflect the idea of a purely territorial economy as a drastically different condition from footloose industries and, in a more general sense, from flow-substitution economies (Storper 1997, 177–181). A *localist approach* is most usual in rural communities and small towns, echoing the premises of asset-based community development (McKnight and Kretzmann 1990), amenity-based community development (Green 2001), or the economics of amenity (McNulty 1988). Among wellness sectors such approaches have a tendency to give weight to natural attractions, 3S (spas, springs, and saunas), fitness clubs, and wellness lifestyle real estate, all firmly tied to local community.

Some of the cities in the Western world rely for their development on an urban growth management strategy premised on such features as consumption-orientation, compactness, livability, and quality of life (e.g. Allen 2015). Levine (2015), for example, has concluded that in the global age, localist machine-style practices have ceded way to a new political culture in which municipal leaders and developers emphasize the effective provision of public services, improvements in the quality of life, and the importance of urban amenities to attracting economic activities to a city. Such a view reflects a paradigm shift in economic development, for the emphasis in understanding the premises of urban economic development has evolved from the primacy of the factors of production, production function, and exports, to the importance of urban amenities, consumption, and visitor attraction (Clark 2011; Anttiroiko 2014). For example, *high amenity cities* have grown faster than low amenity cities (Glaeser et al. 2001) and access to shops are obviously conducive to the attractiveness of cities (Öner 2017). Concerning wellness, in the development of a consumer city with the special role of offering urban amenities, attention is naturally paid to boutiques, salons, spa hotels, and studios that offer beauty and anti-aging products and services as well as retail business that sell products relating to healthy diet, nutrition, and weight loss.

A drastically different approach from the previous ones are the export-base theory of urban-regional growth and the theorization of attraction-oriented economic development, which see the city at the outset as a hub of global economic flows and essentially as export machines—at least if the city strives for economic growth (Florida et al. 2016; Anttiroiko 2015). It emphasizes the need to attract investment and talent, and other critical factors for production, and to create favorable conditions for innovation-driven exports (e.g. SPUR 2010). Such an approach favors both attraction and export functions of an urban dissipative structure. Wellness tourism is a prime example of a wellness-focused attraction strategy, while exporting innovative wellness products and equipment serves as an example of an export-oriented strategy. These strategies are discussed further in Chap. 6.

Wellness Asset Analysis

Local asset analysis categorizes and values local assets to provide the critical knowledge needed in the planning of wellness-oriented economic development. Concerning available frameworks and methods in place marketing, four place-based categories have been identified as key attractors:

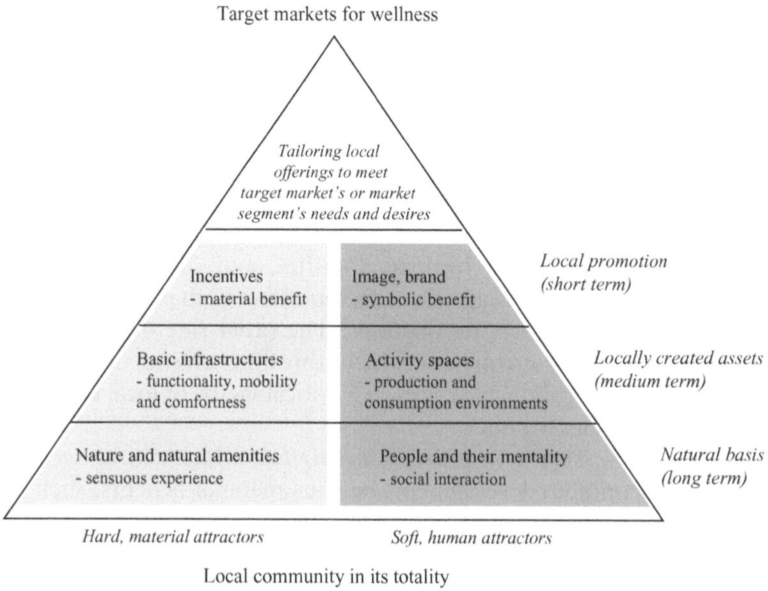

Fig. 4.2 Local asset categories in economic development. (Source: Modified from Anttiroiko 2015)

infrastructure, attractions, people, and images (Kotler et al. 1993). Another framework is the balanced local attractor model, which includes three levels divided into hard and soft sides, as presented in Fig. 4.2. This is one way of mapping out the major local assets that can be used to analyze the city's prerequisites for wellness-focused development.

It goes without saying that *nature* is a fundamental element of wellness, not least because it is the original human habitat and essential for human life. Climate, for example, has a tremendous effect on people's movements, relocation, and travel. Interestingly, a large portion of weather-related movement appears to be driven by an increased valuation of nice weather as a kind of consumption amenity (Rappaport 2007). In general, natural assets such as beautiful landscapes, forest sounds, and the element of water have been fundamental for retreats, springs, and spas for centuries and are self-evidently a cornerstone of wellness tourism.

Another natural basis for wellness development is *local people*, which is worth a closer look when concerned with wellness-focused economic development. Are locals known for being friendly, warm, and hospitable? Are there healing, massage, or spiritual traditions that would attract wellness tourists? For instance, Indonesian people have a tradition of living in harmony and they support well-being through herbs, water, thermal resources, music, dance, meditation, prayer, and traditional medicine, which has created conducive conditions for wellness development (Hutagalung Budidharma 2014).

Another important category is *locally created assets*, which include basic infrastructure, environmental hygiene, logistics, and similar aspects of urban functionality and comfort. These factors affect both perceived desirability and access to wellness destinations. The other side of the coin is *man-made facilities and attractions*, which, through investments in wellness destinations and production sites, is a critical factor of local development strategy and cluster policy.

Lastly, there are *short-term promotion activities*, which can be seen as assets in local economic development, be they material benefits, such as incentives to footloose firms, or images or brands that are used to appeal to selected target groups (Anttiroiko 2015).

If we want to emphasize *actors and institutions* in asset analysis, we can deepen that dimension using an asset-based community development (ABCD) model. Even if ABCD aims to build and utilize local capacity and expand social capital, it recognizes that disadvantaged communities may also seek assistance from outside the community, which is most effectively used when a community's own assets are leveraged at full capacity (McKnight and Kretzmann 1990). ABCD can reverse internalized powerlessness, strengthen opportunities for collective endeavors, and help to build local capacity for action (Mathie et al. 2017). According to ABCD, five assets that are worth special attention in any given community are individuals, associations, institutions, physical assets, and connections (Kretzmann and McKnight 1993), as described in Fig. 4.3.

Local assets play a decisive role in understanding a city's economic profile. Local asset analysis is, however, only a beginning. It needs to be incorporated into strategic planning, cluster identification, and smart specialization. Local assets and location-specific factors have a vital role in such planning, even though it is equally important to pay attention to the adjustment oflocality to its economic environment (European Commission 2013). Let us next shed light on cluster policy, which builds a relational picture of wellness-oriented local economic development (Robinson 2015).

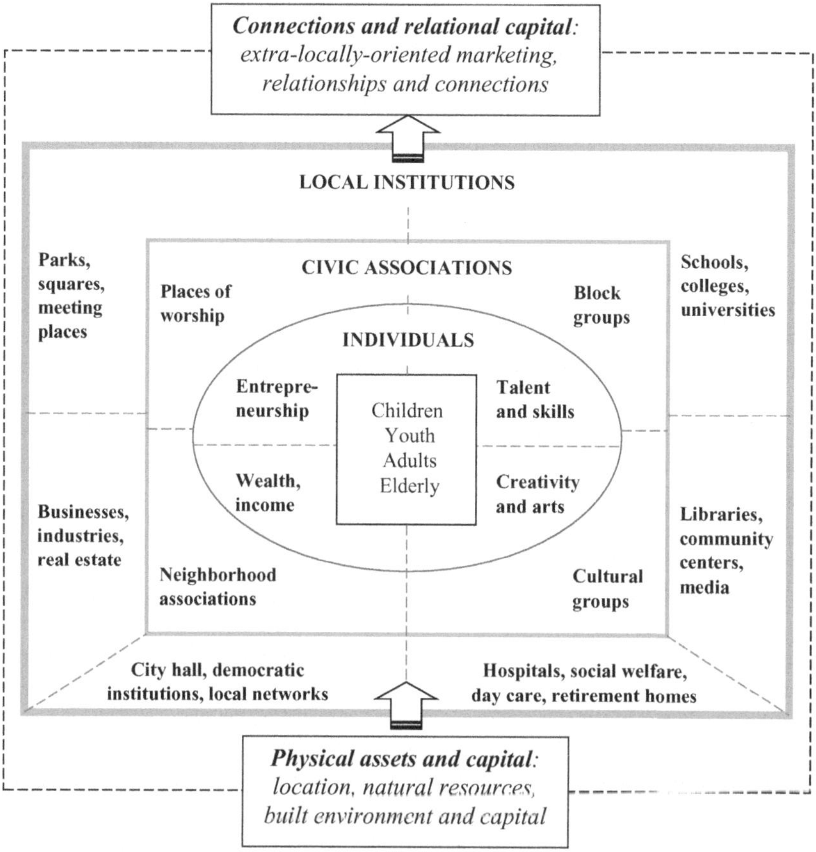

Fig. 4.3 Community assets map. (Source: Modified from Kretzmann and McKnight 1993)

Wellness in Local Cluster Policy

Focusing on wellness in local economic development is a choice, just like any other local policy decision. Thus, local decision-makers and public managers should ask themselves whether it would be beneficial for a city to promote a wellness cluster instead of some other industry or cluster. This challenge can be approached with both a broad and a narrow focus. The former implies an incorporation of wellness into integrative urban development planning and revitalization, while the latter has a sharper focus on building and supporting a wellness cluster, that is, a geographic concentration of interconnected firms and related actors, such as specialized service providers, universities, and intermediary organizations (OECD 2010). In this chapter, we apply a narrow interpretation to shed light on wellness through the lens of conventional cluster policy.

Interconnectedness is an inherent feature of *clusters*, yet there is a new generation of cluster policies that connect unrelated activities around a common theme (van Winden and de Carvalho 2015). Such an approach fits well with the idea of a wellness city. Such a *thematic cluster policy* opens up new opportunities for economic diversification that makes use of specific local strengths, such as gastronomy, hospitality, natural resources, or engineering skills, or of global networks and connections, as in the utilization of globally distributed knowledge, digital platforms, and innovation networks (Anttiroiko 2015). On the basis of their case study on San Sebastian's surf cluster, van Winden and de Carvalho (2015) concluded that nurturing an economy around a theme or lifestyle requires an integrated platform approach, the flexibility of intervention, and occasionally also the involvement of "unusual" stakeholders.

Some guidance for cluster policy is given by Michael E. Porter. An important advice, when applied to wellness, is to be cautious about betting on wellness if the city does not have any historical roots or particular competitive advantages in this field. As Porter (1998) pointed out, "[g]overnment, working with the private sector, should reinforce and build on existing and emerging clusters rather than attempt to create entirely new ones." It is also good to keep in mind that largely for the same reason cluster formation should be approached as an evolutionary process, acknowledging that most clusters form independently of government intervention where a foundation of locational advantages exists (Porter 1998).

Another of Porter's (1998) normative views is that cluster development initiatives should embrace the pursuit of competitive advantage and specialization rather than imitating successful cases. This implies that it is wise to build actions on conditions, factors, or attractors that are location-specific or strongly localized. Such a choice can simply be more effective than head-on competition with well-established rival cities. The two interrelated preconditions are:

- A city has a *competitive advantage* if it is in a better position than its competitor due to some factors available to it or due to some of its features or conditions in terms of given criteria, such as capital inflow, income generation, growth rate, or other desirable outcome.

- In the context of local economic policy, *specialization* is a policy choice when the city government chooses to promote a limited number of industries in order to achieve optimal gain in terms of investment, employment, and economic growth, which leads to division of labor between producer cities.

These considerations help to assess whether focusing on selected wellness industries or a broadly defined wellness cluster would be a viable option for the city (on normative views and recommendations for cluster policy, see OECD 2010; European Commission 2016). At a concrete level, local governments may follow conventional practices of cluster identification and selection, and weigh how much they value, for example, the level of salaries, employment base, export intensity, location quotient, and expected local, national, or international growth (e.g. Economics Center for Education and Research 2004). Such choices lead to a selection of industries or clusters, to which the city directs its development efforts, as evident in the development of: Kobe Biomedical Innovation Cluster in the city of Kobe in Japan; the Green Tech Valley as a hotspot of green technology in Graz in Austria; medical technology cluster in the town of Tuttlingen in the southwest of Germany; or the concentration of biotechnology, pharmaceutical, and medical device industries in San Francisco Bay Area, California.

Without going into detail on the design and implementation of local wellness-oriented cluster policy, there is a need to remember that when shaping development policy *local wellness regime* has to take into account three interrelated points: (1) the integrated policy framework for local economic development; (2) the requirements of a wellness-oriented cluster policy and specialization, and (3) the co-ordination of the independently managed and developed major wellness destinations in the area. An overall city strategy must guide local cluster policy, which supports the activities of wellness institutions and businesses. In the same way, city-wide place-shaping efforts should be integrated with wellness-oriented cluster formations, which again is related to the management of major local wellness destinations (See Dvorak et al. 2014).

References

Allen, N. (2015). Understanding the Importance of Urban Amenities: A Case Study from Auckland. *Buildings, 5*, 85–99.

Ancarani, F., & Gisco, A. (Eds.). (2014). *Wellness Marketing: New Strategies for New Trends*. Milan: Egea.

Anttiroiko, A.-V. (2014). *The Political Economy of City Branding*. London: Routledge.
Anttiroiko, A.-V. (2015). *New Urban Management: Attracting Value Flows to Branded Hubs*. Basingstoke: Palgrave Macmillan.
Blair, J. P., & Carroll, M. C. (2009). *Local Economic Development: Analysis, Practices, and Globalization* (2nd ed.). London: Sage.
Castells, M. (1997). *The Power of Identity. The Information Age: Economy, Society, and Culture, Volume II*. Oxford: Blackwell.
Clark, T. N. (Ed.). (2011). *The City as an Entertainment Machine*. Lanham: Lexington Books.
Dvorak, D., Saari, S., & Tuominen, T. (Eds.). (2014). *Developing a Competitive Health and Well-Being Destination*. Turku: Turku University of Applied Sciences.
Economics Center for Education and Research. (2004). *Identification of Industry Clusters for Guiding Economic Development Efforts in Cincinnati USA*. Prepared for the Cincinnati USA Partnership, 19 May. Retrieved August 12, 2017, from http://docplayer.net/20976689-Identification-of-industry-clusters-for-guiding-economic-development-efforts-in-cincinnati-usa.html
European Commission. (2013). *The Role of Clusters and Smart Specialization Strategies*. Directorate-General for Research and Innovation. Retrieved August 17, 2017, from https://ec.europa.eu/research/evaluations/pdf/archive/other_reports_studies_and_documents/clusters_smart_spec2013.pdf
European Commission. (2016). *Smart Guide to Cluster Policy*. Ref. Ares(2016)2507138—31/05/2016. Retrieved August 17, 2017, from http://s3platform.jrc.ec.europa.eu/documents/20182/84453/Smart+Guide+to+Cluster+Policy/fd0f16b9-0759-43ca-b950-ec0192e220c8
Florida, R., Adler, P., & Mellander, C. (2016). *The City as Innovation Machine*. Ref. 2016-MPIWP-002. Martin Prosperity Institute, University of Toronto. Retrieved August 17, 2016, form http://martinprosperity.org/media/2016-MPIWP-002_The-City-as-Innovation-Machine_Florida-Adler-Mellander.pdf
Giddens, A. (1992). *The Consequences of Modernity*. Cambridge: Polity Press.
Glaeser, E. L., Kolko, J., & Saiz, A. (2001). Consumer City. *Journal of Economic Geography, 1*(1), 27–50.
GWI. (2017, January). *Global Wellness Economy Monitor*. Miami: Global Wellness Institute.
Green, G. P. (2001). Amenities and Community Economic Development: Strategies for Sustainability. *The Journal of Regional Analysis & Policy, 31*(2), 61–75.
Green Carmichael, S.(2012, March 16). Why "Generation Why Bother" Doesn't Care. *Harvard Business Review*. Retrieved September 10, 2017, from https://hbr.org/2012/03/americas-jobs-and-wages-proble

Hueltenschmidt, N., Olsen, T., & Vishwanath, V. (2013, May 6). *Healthy Living: Economic Necessity and Business Opportunity*. Bain Industry Brief. Bain & Company. Retrieved September 16, 2017, from http://www.bain.com/publications/articles/healthy-living-economic-necessity-and-business-opportunity.aspx

Hutagalung Budidharma, L. (2014). Indonesia—Spices and Well-being in the Archipelago of Wonder. Weltest Case Study 4. In D. Dvorak, S. Saari, & T. Tuominen (Eds.), *Developing a Competitive Health and Well-Being Destination* (pp. 52–54). Turku: Turku University of Applied Sciences.

Inglehart, R. (1977). *The Silent Revolution: Changing Values and Political Styles among Western Publics*. Princeton: Princeton University Press.

Jouen, M., Kolosy, K., Pellegrin, J.-P., Ramsden, P., Szegvari, P., & Chambon, N. (2010). *Cohesion Policy Support for Local Development: Best Practice and Future Policy Options* (Final Report. CCI n.2009.CE.16.0.AT.081). Brussels: Directorate General for Regional Policy, European Commission. Retrieved August 18, 2017, from http://ec.europa.eu/regional_policy/archive/consultation/terco/cp_support_local_dev_en.pdf

Kotler, P., Haider, D. H., & Rein, I. (1993). *Marketing Places: Attracting Investment, Industry, and Tourism to Cities, States, and Nations*. New York: The Free Press.

Kresl, P. K., & Fry, E. H. (2005). *The Urban Response to Internationalization*. Cheltenham: Edward Elgar.

Kretzmann, J., & McKnight, J. (1993). *Building Communities from the Inside Out: A Path Toward Finding and Mobilizing a Community's Assets* (3rd ed.). Chicago: ACTA Publications.

Lash, S. & Urry, J. (2007). *The End of Organized Capitalism*. First Published 1987. Cambridge: Polity Press.

Leigh, N. G., & Blakely, E. J. (2013). *Planning Local Economic Development: Theory and Practice* (5th ed.). London: Sage.

Levine, M. A. (2015). *Urban Politics: Cities and Suburbs in a Global Age* (9th ed.). New York: Routledge.

Lyotard, J.-F. (1984). *The Postmodern Condition: A Report on Knowledge* (G. Bennington & B. Massumi, trans.). Original Title: *La Condition postmoderne: rapport sur le savoir*, published in 1979. Manchester: Manchester University Press.

Mathie, A., Cameron, J., & Gibson, K. (2017). Asset-Based and Citizen-Led Development: Using a Diffracted Power Lens to Analyze the Possibilities and Challenges. *Progress in Development Studies, 17*(1), 54–66.

McKnight, J. L., & Kretzmann, J. P. (1990). *Mapping Community Capacity*. Evanston: Center for Urban Affairs and Policy Research, Northwestern University. Retrieved August 17, 2017, from https://mn.gov/mnddc/parallels2/pdf/90s/90/90-MCC-McKnight_Kretzmann.pdf

McMurray, A., & Clendon, J. (2015). *Community Health and Wellness: Primary Health Care in Practice* (5th ed.). Chatswood: Elsevier.

McNulty, R. (1988). The Economics of Amenity. *Meanjin, 47*(4), 614–624. Retrieved August 18, 2017, from http://search.informit.com.au/documentSummary;dn=582268386651646;res=IELLCC

OECD. (2001). *Best Practices in Local Development.* Local Economic and Employment Development (LEED). Paris: OECD.

OECD. (2010). *Cluster Policies.* OECD Innovation Policy Platform. Last Updated: January 2010. Retrieved August 17, 2017, from http://www.oecd.org/innovation/policyplatform/48137710.pdf

Öner, Ö. (2017). Retail City: The Relationship Between Place Attractiveness and Accessibility to Shops. *Spatial Economic Analysis, 12*(1), 72–91.

Pilzer, P. Z. (2007). *The New Wellness Revolution: How to Make a Fortune in the Next Trillion Dollar Industry?* (2nd ed.). Hoboken: John Wiley & Sons.

Porter, M. E. (1998). Clusters and the New Economics of Competition. *Harvard Business Review, 76*(6), 77–90.

Rappaport, J. (2007). Moving to Nice Weather. *Regional Science and Urban Economics, 37*(3), 375–398.

Robinson, D. J. (2015, August 6). *Economic Cluster Analysis Capitalizes on Local Assets in Growing Markets.* The Montrose Group, LLC. Retrieved August 17, 2017, from http://montrosegroupllc.com/economic-cluster-analysis-capitalizes-on-local-assets-in-growing-markets/

SPUR. (2010). *Organizing for Economic Growth: A New Approach to Business Attraction and Retention in San Francisco.* SPUR Report, July 15, 2009. Released June, 2010. San Francisco: San Francisco Planning + Urban Research Association (SPUR).

Stewart, J. (1983). *Local Government: The Conditions of Local Choice.* London/Boston: Allen & Unwin.

Storper, M. (1997). *The Regional World. Territorial Development in a Global Economy.* New York/London: The Guilford Press.

Toffler, A. (1970). *Future Shock.* New York: Random House.

van Winden, W., & de Carvalho, L. (2015, April). *New Style Cluster Policy: Riding the Waves of San Sebastian's Emerging Surf Economy.* URBACT II Capitalisation. Saint Denis: URBACT. Retrieved August 17, 2017, from http://urbact.eu/sites/default/files/cs-01a_nu-sansebastian-f5.pdf

CHAPTER 5

Dimensions of the Wellness City

Abstract This chapter drills down into the eight dimensions of the Y model of wellness and their relevance for urban economic development: health care as a wellness-related business; spa, beauty, and fitness as the soft core of a wellness cluster; wellness-related shopping, entertainment, and human desires; natural assets and livable urban environments; life sciences and wellness technologies as high value-added activities; local facilitation of intellectuality and learning; cultural experiences, sociability, and play; and lastly, meditation, spirituality, and transcendence. These dimensions point to activity areas of vital importance for holistic health that can be systematically developed and utilized in the revitalization of a local economy, talent and investment attraction, and job creation.

Keywords Health care • Spa • Fitness • Livability • Wellness technology • Spirituality

The previous chapters discussed wellness and its relevance to the development of urban economies. This chapter drills deeper into various dimensions of wellness. The structure of this chapter draws from the wellness city typology presented in Chap. 2 and elaborates each dimension of the model by focusing on its basic features and development potentials. The idea is to assess the economic potential of the most important aspects of the wellness city paradigm and show their forms, synergies, and relevance

A.-V. Anttiroiko, *Wellness City*,
https://doi.org/10.1007/978-3-319-75562-5_5

with special regard to *locality development* anchored in locally fixed or slowly changing assets and determinants, such as location, natural assets, infrastructure, and population (on local economic development, see Blakely and Bradshaw 2002).

Workplace wellness is deliberately left out of the discussion as a separate category, as is also wellness tourism, as they can be seen as cross-cutting themes, that is, they relate to several dimensions of wellness. The former operates essentially at company level, and is thus not in our focus in spite of its connection with community health, while the latter as an integrated view of the activity of traveling motivated by wellness encompasses practically all the dimensions elaborated in this section. Both of these areas are among the most widely discussed aspects of the wellness industry and are fairly well covered in current literature, which makes their separate discussion here unnecessary (see e.g. Gatchel and Schultz 2012; Smith and Puczkó 2009). However, as wellness and medical tourism is a focal area in integrative wellness city development, Chap. 6 addresses it separately as a significant form of attraction-oriented wellness city strategy.

Health Care as a Wellness Business

While public health forms a natural part of the wellness industry, the health care system as a whole is systematically excluded in wellness discourse due to its "illness care" focus. However, from the point of view of local economic development this demarcation is largely unfit. Thus, in this book we perceive health care and wellness as unified sector that deals with entire *health continuum* that ranges from reactive medical cure to preventive holistic health and, in case there is a need to emphasize the medical side of this marriage, refer to it with the term *wellness+*.

Let us start with one of the most important premises of health care, which was formulated by Asch and Volpp (2012) as follows: "doctors and hospitals focus on producing health care, what people really want is health. Health care is just a means to that end—and an increasingly expensive one. If we could get better health some other way, just as we can now produce images without film and transport people and freight without railroads, then maybe we wouldn't have to rely so much on health care" (p. 888). The current literature supports the view that differences in health are determined as much by the *social circumstances* that underlie them as by the biological processes that mediate them. This neither deems health care as an unimportant determinant of health nor does it deny the fact that health care is among the most easily modifiable determinants. That is, it has been easier to establish systems to support the writing of prescriptions and the performance of surgery than to cure poverty, prevent social exclusion, or relieve segregation. Nevertheless, the evidence suggests that health care as conventionally delivered explains only a small number of premature deaths as compared with other factors, such as social context, environmental influences, and personal behavior. This implies that organizations in the business of delivering health need to take a broader view of health and expand their offerings (Asch and Volpp 2012).

An issue that points in the same direction is that many of the conditions driving the need for treatment are *preventable*. This means that we should pay special attention to those policy issues that help prevent disease or promote health. There is a need to review the variety of the determinants of population health—genetic predispositions, social circumstances, environmental conditions, behavioral patterns, and medical care—and to analyze the factors inhibiting policy attention and resource commitment to the non-medical determinants of population health (McGinnis et al. 2002).

Previous discussion hints that the road from conventional health care system to wellness goes through *public health*. Public health refers to the health of the population as a whole, especially as monitored, regulated, and promoted by the government (Oxford Dictionaries 2017). It is the science of protecting the safety and improving the health of a population through education, policy making, and research on disease and injury prevention. It includes tasks such as: monitoring the health status of a community to identify potential problems; diagnosing and investigating health problems and hazards in the community; informing, educating, and empowering people about health issues, particularly the underserved and those at risk; and mobilizing community partnerships to identify and solve health problems. This points to the critical difference between trained physicians and those working in public health, for the former treat people who are sick, while the latter try to prevent people from getting sick or injured in the first place (APHA 2017; Baggott 2011).

Public health activities organized at local level are called *community health* or community wellness (Clark 2002), which emphasize the health-promoting features of the community, including: the presence of strong social capital; engaged and empowered community members; a dynamic and healthy physical, social, and spiritual environment; accessible, affordable, and equitable services and resources; and a system of governance that is inclusive and responsive to community members in addressing the social determinants of health (McMurray and Clendon 2015). Just as communities have a certain level of human and social capital, they can also do well or poorly with ***health capital*** measured by the general health conditions of the local inhabitants and workforce, the effectiveness of the work of local or regional health institutions, and the support provided by urban infrastructures. A vital part of community health is a responsibility of companies, known as workplace or *occupational wellness* (Gatchel and Schultz 2012).

Lifestyle and environment have a tremendous impact on people's health, which has urged public health professionals to take an integrative view of this issue. As crystallized by Troutman and Benjamin (2013, 1),

> re-shaping people's economic, physical, social, and service environments can help ensure opportunities for health and support healthy behaviors. But health and public health agencies rarely have the mandate, authority, or organizational capacity to make these changes. Responsibility for the social determinants of health falls to many non-traditional health partners, such as housing, transportation, education, air quality, parks, criminal justice, energy, and employment agencies. Solutions to our complex and urgent problems will require collaborative efforts across many sectors and all levels, including government agencies, businesses, and community-based organizations.

This urges public health agencies and service providers to work with those who are best positioned to initiate policies and practices that promote healthy environments and create synergies, and who are thus able to benefit simultaneously various socio-economic groups in the local community. Such an approach is called *Health in All Policies*. It is described in the World Health Organization's Adelaide Statement on Health in All Policies as a scheme that assists local leaders and policymakers to integrate considerations of health, well-being, and equity during the development, implementation, and evaluation of policies and services. Such an approach builds on collaborative public health work (Rudolph et al. 2013).

Let us highlight some health care-related issues in the context of a wellness city policy. First, health care is an economically huge sector that satisfies fundamental human needs and is an essential policy and service sector in every advanced country. It is an internally diverse sector, which can provide opportunities for local production and consumption as well as for attracting investments and visitor flows from outside the community. In the wide sense of the word, health care markets include such areas as health care finance, professional education, professional and institutional health care services, health care products, health care technologies, and other input factor markets (on health care markets, see e.g. Gaynor and Town 2011; Gaynor et al. 2017). Key components of a health economy are described in Fig. 5.1.

Second, an important point to keep in mind is the role of hospitals and other *health care institutions* in local development. They not only have special responsibilities in health care but also provide development potentials due to their connection with surrounding communities. For instance, they can contribute to cluster and district formation in the area, as in the cases of the Vita Health and Wellness District, which improves the health and resilience of the neighborhood surrounding Stamford Hospital in Stamford, Connecticut (Vita Health and Wellness District 2013), or the Flint Health and Wellness District in downtown Flint, Michigan (Schuch 2015).

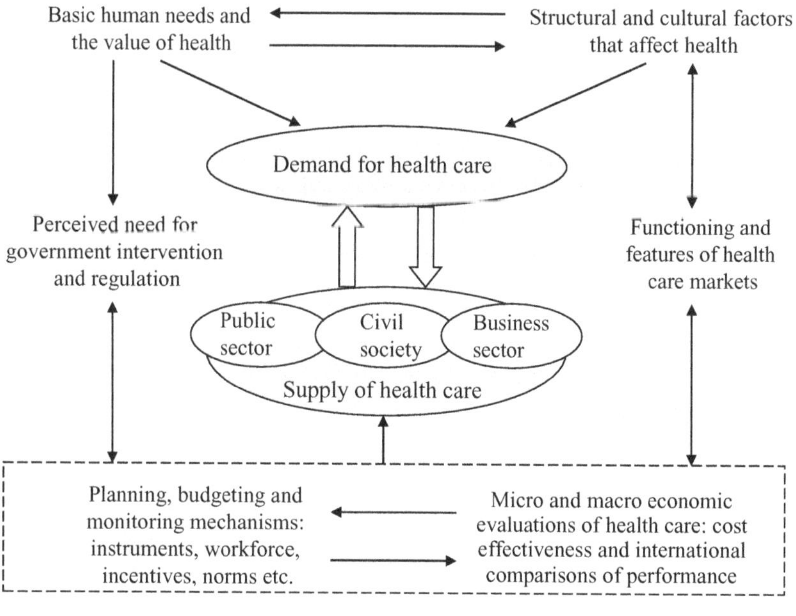

Fig. 5.1 Aspects of health economics. (Source: Modified from Williams 1987)

Third, one of the most critical issues from the point of view of the development of a wellness industry is to determine its relationship with established health care systems, which boils down to the issue of *service integration*. These two areas have some natural intersections in public health and community health as well as in therapeutic recreation, rehabilitation, and occupational wellness (Dvorak et al. 2014; Smith and Puczkó 2009). An integrative approach to health and wellness incorporates "hard," or conventional, medicine with *complementary and alternative medicine* to the degree that there is evidence of the health benefits brought about by their complementary roles and synergies. Alternative medicine refers to the family of therapies and healing that are not regarded as orthodox by the medical profession, nor included in the traditional curricula taught in medical schools (e.g. herbalism, homeopathy, chiropractic, naturopathy, or Ayurveda), while complementary medicine is generally seen as more acceptable in this respect, such as acupuncture and osteopathy, and thus can be used alongside conventional medicine (cf. Oxford Dictionaries 2017). Such complementary and alternative therapies are usually included in the service packages of full-service wellness centers.

The idea of integration relates to a revolutionary shift from medical to wellness paradigm, which is crystallized in the idea that a *wellness center* is the hospital of the twenty-first century (Gallup 1999). The story of modern wellness centers dates back to the 1970s, one of the pioneers being Cooper Aerobics Center in Houston, Texas. The Riverside Health System in Newport News, Virginia, was another landmark in the early 1980s by starting one of the first wellness center programs. Gottlieb Hospital in Melrose Park, Illinois, created the nation's first freestanding wellness center facility, followed by Sports Med Center for Fitness, and soon after the Garter Life Center's freestanding urban center, both in a Chicago suburb. From the early 1970s until the late 1990s some 350 centers were built, and the number multiplied in the following decades (Gallup 1999). Around the same time, many spas rebranded themselves as wellness destinations and added conventional, alternative, or complementary medical treatments to their service palettes, which further strengthened the de facto integration of medicine and wellness.

Fourth, technological developments, data science, and the emerging paradigm shift in medicine dramatically affected health care and wellness and their integration. *Systems medicine*, which is a special medical application of systems biology, has spurred a paradigm shift in medicine towards *precision medicine*, which is built on improved capabilities of obtaining genomic information. Hence, the widely used term *post-genomic era*, which depicts the nature of this medical revolution. Its ultimate promise is a transition from reactive disease care towards predictive, preventive, personalized, and participatory medicine, these four functions being grouped under the label *P4 medicine*. Such P4 medicine is supposed to be holistic rather than reductionist, steps taken seemingly towards holistic wellness. As explained by Torrance (2011), "[i]n the future, however, we will have the ability to rationally prescribe and adapt the right drug, drug combination, or drug dose, to each patient based on having a detailed understanding of their disease genetics, to far more effectively manage their disease." However, rather than representing a medical holism associated with humanistically oriented holistic health, an alternative techno-scientific holism may be in the making, a kind of "holistic medicalization" that implies our whole life process is defined in biomedical and techno-scientific terms as quantifiable and controllable and is underlaid by a regime of medical control. Thus, while such developments are likely to improve health risk assessment and diagnosis, they may have many unintended consequences. This may paradoxically require that, in the name of holistic wellness, we search for a new level of preventive measures to avoid overmedicalization through systems medicine (Vogt et al. 2016; Vilhelmsson 2017). One way of validating medical innovations and assessing their long-term consequences and, with regard to the previously raised concerns, securing that P4 medicine benefits the overall health of people and their communities in an optimal way, is their assessment within the framework of holistic and integrative community health and wellness.

Fifth, there are plenty of opportunities to expand health care services into niche markets. Both complementary and alternative medicine are obvious niche markets, as is the introduction of medical treatments to spa environments. Another potential area is known as the *silver economy*. Developed countries are aging because the share of older people is increasing due to declining fertility rates and rising life expectancy. Such a development provides economic opportunities arising from the public and consumer expenditure related to population aging and the specific needs of senior citizens. It is worth noting that with regard to economic sectors, the silver economy revolves around wellness, as sectors that are expected to benefit from its rise include cosmetics and fashion, tourism, smart homes, service robotics, health (including medical devices, pharmaceuticals, and e-health), safety, culture, education and skills, entertainment, personal and autonomous transport, banking, and relevant financial products (European Commission 2015).

There are also challenging or controversial niche markets that are worth a closer look from the point of view of local economic development, one of them being *euthanasia* as a person's last act of freedom and self-determination. Our right to end our own lives in a decent and socially acceptable manner, especially in the case of terminal illness, is a fundamental issue of wellness, which is explicitly granted in only a few countries and under a strict set of conditions, allowing for passive euthanasia (withdrawing treatment), assisted suicide, or active euthanasia. It is a paradox that still today more than half of the world's population live in countries that allow capital punishment, but euthanasia is a taboo and thus extremely difficult for authoritative political institutions to accept. The Netherlands was the first country to legalize euthanasia and assisted suicide in the early 2000s, soon followed by Belgium. Some forms of active euthanasia or assisted suicide are also possible in Germany, Switzerland, Luxembourg, Colombia, Canada, and a few US states. Due to the few places where active euthanasia is legal, some cities have become final destinations for *suicide tourism*, one of them being Zurich, the largest city in Switzerland—between 2008 and 2012 more than 600 people from 31 countries, the majority from Germany and the UK, went to Switzerland for assisted suicide (Wilson 2014). In fact, "going to Switzerland" became a euphemism for assisted suicide. In all, this is an example of a niche market that is a natural part of an integrative wellness city policy. Such a policy is supposed to support local service developments and innovations that have a potential to meet the demand for niche services. It is worth keeping in mind that the matter in question is primarily about human rights and self-determination, and only after that about legal provision and, as a last instance, about medical social control.

Previous discussion should have made it clear that health care is not only about illness and specialized "illness care" institutions, nor should it be seen only as an economic burden (see e.g. Williams 1987). It forms a considerable share of the local economy, has a deep impact on a city's economic performance, and provides a plethora of business opportunities. For instance, the health science institutions of the Medical District in the Near Southside in Fort Worth have been essential partners in the area's revitalization. In addition, their impact extends far beyond the neighborhood. A 2014 University of North Texas study of the Medical District's health care providers stated that they accounted for nearly 39,000 jobs, and their facilities documented a USD 4.2 billion annual economic impact in Fort Worth, and USD 5.5 billion in the wider Tarrant County (Near Southside, Inc. n/a).

Packham and others (2006) analyzed the impact of local health care systems on the Humboldt County economy. They provided sufficient evidence to claim that the local health care sector has a substantial impact on income, employment, and sales tax revenue in the area, which is often overlooked in public policy discussions of health care costs, access to care, and community benefits. They concluded that "[t]he health sector plays a critical role in local economic development by creating jobs and income for residents of Humboldt County through the normal operations of hospitals and other health-related enterprises. The health sector is also responsible for generating employment and income in other businesses in the community." (Packham et al. 2006, 1).

As the preceding suggests, the existence of a strong health care system plays a critical role in local economic development by attracting business, industry, and retirees, and by generating jobs and payroll in its own right. However, probably the most important economic role the health sector plays in local economy is "keeping local health care dollars at home." Employees in the health service sector get higher than average wages and are an important segment in local household consumption. Hospitals and other health sector establishments are also important purchasers of local goods and services that are needed in the provision of health care, including laundry and waste management (Packham et al. 2006).

To sum up, what can we say about the general relevance of health care in terms of business potential, job creation, diversification of economic bases, and locality development in the context of a comprehensive wellness city policy? First and foremost, hospital, medical, and dental activities (Wellness+), together with health-related technological development, innovation, and scientific research (Wellness++) form a high-value-adding part of the wellness economy, which has already emerged as a spearhead of wellness strategies in many major cities, providing opportunities for both producer and consumer cities. The following measures are instrumental for exploiting such an opportunity: (1) integrating traditional welfare and health care with wellness industries within a creative, integrative, and entrepreneurial wellness cluster policy; (2) utilizing structural health care reforms in making a paradigm shift towards holistic health and wellness and, along with it, creating opportunities for responsible wellness businesses through outsourcing, partnerships, and consumer choice; (3) creating geographical clusters for the special benefits of agglomeration, as in the cases of university hospital complexes or pharmaceutical and biomedical industrial clusters; and (4) applying open-minded R&D, innovation, and technology development efforts to health care and wellness. This approach contributes to a strategic gain through cluster formation and dedicated efforts to utilize globalization and technological development, which have already started to revolutionize both health care and wellness industries.

Spa, Beauty, and Fitness

We can fairly say that the soft core of a wellness cluster is the trinity of spa, beauty, and fitness. They all comprise specialized services, products, technologies, shops, and destinations—for example Willow Stream Spa in Vancouver, Canada; John Barret Salon at Fifth Avenue in New York; or CityFitness gyms in New Zealand—and often work in different combinations or as integrated destinations, such as an integrated spa, beauty, grooming, and fitness center at One&Only Palmilla luxury resort in Los Cabos, Mexico. This trinity forms about half of all narrowly defined wellness businesses (Global Wellness Institute 2017).

In previous centuries, *spa* was a common designation for a resort with mineral springs where visitors could take the cure. A number of spa resorts are still genuine spas with mineral springs. There are also many spa towns and cities that are known for their mineral springs and hydrotherapies, such as Spa in Belgium, Bath in the UK, or Baden-Baden in Germany, a latecomer is Reykjavik in Iceland. In due course, spas started to offer auxiliary services while various beauty parlors and wellness salons wanted to become associated with spa treatments and facilities without the involvement of a natural water element, which gradually led to the broad conception of a modern-era spa. Thus, today spa means a place to receive massages, facials, body scrubs, and other services in either a day or overnight setting (Brown 2017). This is in line with the rather broad definition of spa offered by the International Spa Association, which defines spas as "places devoted to enhancing overall well-being through a variety of professional services that encourage the renewal of mind, body and spirit." A spa is a place where people go to improve their physical health, appearance, weight loss, fitness, and/or to relax. Most conventional facilities are water-based spas, resort spas, and thermal springs, but they also include day and hotel spas and a large number of specialized facilities (Ellis 2017;

Erfurt-Cooper and Cooper 2009). The spa economy has been growing steadily in terms of the number of spa facilities, revenues, and employment. The most important categories of spas are day, hotel, and resort spas, which are most numerous in Europe and Asia-Pacific (see Cohen and Bodeker 2008).

Wellness opportunities for the traditional spa industry is in helping to reshape their image and to move away from a perception of them as mere providers of luxurious pampering and beauty services for the wealthy. This reflects a transition from mindless to mindful spending. Placing spa within the context of holistic health has the potential to raise awareness that massage and other spa services offer real therapeutic benefits beyond pampering, helping consumers to view their spa spending as an investment or an essential element in maintaining their health (GSS 2010).

The opportunities for integrating spas with other areas of urban wellness have many facets, the three most notable being:

- On the reactive/treatment-oriented side of the wellness continuum, spas and wellness centers can bring supplementary wellness-oriented elements to the *medical sector*.
- On the proactive/wellness-oriented side, spas and wellness centers can link with other wellness services, products and activities to help enhance people's health and quality of life. This brings complementary services into spa arena and thus serve as the sites of *wellness integration*.
- Within the realm of *workplace health and wellness*, the spa industry can capitalize on the trend of employers taking seriously the need to improve the health and wellness of their senior executives and other employees (GSS 2010).

Beauty, anti-aging, and personal care is a diverse business sector. It includes consumer products and technologies—makeup, deodorant and nail products, hair care products, creams/lotions, perfumes, mouthwashes, shaving preparations and other products—used for beautification and personal hygiene, and services, service packages, beauty shops, and various service environments. In terms of local amenities and services, beauty and personal care has an essential role through beauty, nail and tanning salons, barbershops, waxing franchises, massage parlors, and luxury spas. Competition in the beauty industry is expanding beyond its conventional borders to include pharmaceutical products, food, and beverages that claim to support skin and hair health, among other body functions. One of the internal wellness-related controversies in this business is the usefulness and safety of the products. The Campaign for Safe Cosmetics, for example, addresses this issue and demands that the cosmetics industry makes safer products (see http://www.safecosmetics.org).

From a location development perspective the *fitness industry* revolves around gyms, health clubs, sports centers, and fitness centers. Fitness refers to businesses that provide infrastructure—such as space, equipment, and training—in exchange for a membership fee. Globally there are over 180,000 fitness centers, estimated to have earned USD 84 billion from a total of 145 million members in the mid-2010s. It means millions of paying gym members, billions of visits per year, and hundreds of thousands of jobs throughout the world (Sena n/a).

An older brother of fitness is *sports*. It is an important mainstream activity in the economy, a market that in North America alone was worth USD 60.5 billion in 2014 and is expected to reach USD 73.5 billion by 2019. In the UK, in the mid-2010s sports was roughly a GBP 20 billion industry, supporting over 450,000 jobs. It generates income from gate revenues (stadiums), media rights deals, sponsorship, and merchandising (Heitner 2015). Interestingly, it is a business that does not have customers in the conventional sense of the word, but fans who support athletes and teams, visit games, watch sports channels, and buy fan products.

Football clubs, ice hockey teams, and other sports teams form a large share of the sports business. Manchester City Football Club, for example, opened a state of the art, GBP 200 million, Etihad campus, a world-class training complex, as part of Sportcity, the largest concentration of sporting venues in Europe close to Manchester city center (see http://sportcity-manchester.com/) (Critchlow 2015). Another indication of their economic significance is that the top football clubs—Manchester (ManU), Barcelona, Real Madrid, Bayern München, Arsenal— many of which are owned by billionaires, are worth USD 2–4.5 billion each and can generate hundreds of millions revenue per year (Ozanian 2017). The two megatrends of our time, globalization and digitalization, are also visible in sports: globalization is seen particularly in sports shows and mega-events, such as Grand Prix Formula 1, Olympic Games, and football World Cups (Andreff 2008); while the application of new technologies in sports varies from smart helmets to tech-assisted refereeing, Internet of Things (IoT) applications, and virtual sport games and betting (Cohen 2016).

It is worth a reminder that governments sponsor recreational activities, exercise, and sports in various ways, including the provision of publicly funded sports and recreation facilities. Sports, exercise, and recreation as a broadly understood economy are not only about world-class football clubs or championship games, but also viable options for supporting both active lifestyles and economic development in middle-sized cities, as in the case of the city of Jyväskylä in Finland.

Jyväskylä is an inland city with some 140,000 inhabitants, located in the middle of forest by Lake Jyväsjärvi, in central Finland. Blessed by a thriving university, University of Jyväskylä, it has been able to develop expertise in sport and health science, and is currently profiling itself as an exercise and well-being hub to reap benefits from the markets for health and well-being technology solutions. Together with a number of partners the city government has started to build a Central Finland Wellness Expertise Cluster relying on two flagship projects. The first one is a versatile indoor sports center in the Hippos sports area, including: existing sports premises; research facilities; a new multi-purpose arena for ice sports, football and concerts; a new exercise center with modifiable spaces for gymnastics, combat and fitness sports, and ball games; a hotel; and other amenities. The number of visitors is expected to grow from 1.6 million visitors per year in the mid-2010s to some 3 to 5 million per year in the early 2020s. Investments in new premises and outdoors areas are estimated to be around euro 300 million. In all, it is expected to be the largest of its kind in the Nordic region when completed in 2020. The other pillar of Jyväskylä'swell-being strategy is Kukkula, a new central hospital dedicated to comprehensive, patient centered, health care, in which prevention and wellness play a central role. Beside clinical facilities, it will include premises for research and business activities that facilitate health care and wellness businesses, innovation, and networking. It will cost about euro 700 million and it is to be completed by 2020 (BusinessJyväskylä n/a).

The *weight loss industry* is not so much about special weight loss centers, as it is about companies developing diet plans, manufacturers of weight-loss supplements, diet book authors, instructors and obesity doctors, and low-fat food and low-calorie soda makers. The global weight loss and weight management market in 2014 was worth around USD 148 billion (Research and Markets 2015). When added to healthy eating, organic food, and other aspects of *nutrition*, its global expenditure was estimated to reach USD 648 billion in the mid-2010s (Global Wellness Institute 2017). This market is considerably affected by the rise of the idea of holistic health, which implies that diet as a standalone issue is being accompanied or even replaced by healthy eating habits and a demand for natural, fresh food (Kell 2015).

What is the general relevance of a combined spa, beauty, and fitness economy in locality development in the context of a comprehensive wellness city policy? In short, this trinity has a special impact on the overall image of the city, as it is associated with comfort, trendiness, and sportiness. It plays a role in health care and wellness integration, in utilizing sports in economic development, and in bringing important added value to local amenities. It also has a vital role in creating wellness districts or quarters as special consumption spaces, even if, so far, branded urban wellness retail and service districts are surprisingly few. Such areas are usually spontaneously developed, as let us say those neighborhoods around North Seventh Street in downtown Phoenix that enjoy a large number of healthy and green-living businesses, retailers, and community organizations (Miron 2017), or a Health & Beauty on Grand Avenue in St. Paul, Minnesota, with beauty shops, salons, beauty lounges, chiropractic offices, day spas, and health care services.

Shopping, Entertainment, and Human Desires

It may be that the most common associations of wellness are with pampering treatments in luxury spas, facial massages in beauty parlors, or meditation in tranquility retreats. These all are high-end services, usually provided on a commercial basis by beauty shops, spa hotels, wellness centers, or resorts. While this impression is correct it is not the whole story. The wellness of people living in cities includes such dimensions of "mind continuum" as adventure, desire, lust, entertainment, self-expression, and happiness (e.g. Benkö et al. 2017), which in an urban context creates connection with the idea of a consumer city or a city as an entertainment machine (Clark 2011). Beside core wellness facilities, cities offer a range of services, activities, and environments that support a hospitality, retail, and entertaining side of urban wellness:

- Shopping: shops, boutiques, malls, and other commercial amenities
- Food and drink: healthy food, gastronomy, catering, bakeries, restaurants, cafés
- Accommodation: resort facilities, hotels, motels, hostels
- Entertainment: concerts, shows, parties, nightlife, nightclubs
- Sexuality: romance, love, intimacy, pornography, prostitution
- Identity and lifestyle: communal living, green lifestyle, naturism, LGBT.

As wellness emerges as a new megatrend it penetrates urban life in many ways. *Shopping* has a strong association with the vanity and excessive consumption of wealthy shopaholics. However, shopping has other faces if seen through the lenses of Zen shopping, retail therapy, and sustainable consumption. Shopping can also contribute to health, happiness, creativity, and self-confidence (Tynan 2008). When looking at production, distribution, retail, and services, it is obvious that a wellness trend is reshaping them all, most notably in such industries as food and beverages and other consumables in the fast-moving consumer goods market, in food services and drinking places, and a range of other service businesses. There are, for instance, healthy hit products, dedicated health cafés, healthy juice bars, good life bakeries, and catering services that bring "wellness on a plate." In the workplace, this wellness is seen in healthy vending machines and cafeteria offerings. Nutrition workshops, cooking classes, TV programs, and similar activities are manifesting the same trend. In short, demand creates business. It is no wonder that the global value of, for example, *healthy foods and drinks* was close to USD 1 trillion in 2017 (Kennell 2016).

A related sign of emerging urban wellness is the penetration of health and wellness in the *retail sector*, which is visible in in-store pharmacies, retail clinics in drug stores or grocery stores, and the incorporation of health and wellness services or programs in retail offerings. While Nike was among the first to organize fitness events in its stores for customers, it seems to be replicated in various forms in a whole variety of wellness-related retail businesses. Wellness has become a new frontier for retailers that increases lifestyle branding, eventfulness at street-level shops, utilization of technology, and inter- and intraindustry integration. If wellness shops used to focus primarily on fashion and beauty, they now provide integrated packages, including wellness events and services, à la the Body Studio in London, which offers everything from a Hemsley and Hemsley food café to a Fit Studio, or Saks and its Fifth Avenue flagship store in New York, which dedicated in 2017 an entire floor to health, beauty, and fitness, called The Wellery—including pop-up classes and events, fitness equipment showrooms, beauty treatments, and a section for fitness apparel brands (WGSN Insider 2017).

Health entertainment can be about health-related entertainment or entertaining health activities (e.g. TV programs, magazines, devices, wellness discos, fitness parties, and health games). Wellness has many connections with the city as an entertainment machine. To start with, having fun with friends and participating in events are manifestations of sociability and enjoyment, and have an obvious connection with wellness. Some cities deliberately brand themselves as sites of leisure and entertainment, which gives them two major options: developing commercial shopping and pampering amenities and personal care services to become a *high amenity city*; or providing venues for sociability, interaction, and events, which takes a turn towards a *party city* or *festival city*. The former is designed to offer pleasure in the shopping amenities and day spas in the city center, while the latter revolves around an attempt to increase livability in the city center or a designated city district, organize events and festivals, and boost partying, clubbing, and nightlife. A combination of these strategies is visible in spas that are becoming more entertaining or are organizing parties in spa or pool environments, as in summer weekend "sparties" or summer night spa parties in Szechenyi Spa & Baths, or winter Magic Bath parties in Lukacs Baths, both in Budapest, Hungary. In general, a gradual integration of wellness, shopping, restaurant and bar industry, and entertainment is a reflection of a transition within cities from space of production to space of consumption that has taken place throughout the developed world (e.g. Wharton et al. 2010).

A special niche profile of party city relies on nightclubs, grassroots music venues, music bars, and novel trends in urban youth culture. *Night culture* benefits many cities economically. Lutz Leichsenring, the spokesperson of Clubcommission Berlin, has mentioned that club culture is important for cities like Berlin in terms of tourism, economy, and culture. For about ten years, the Commission had to work simply to get recognition of *clubbing* as important to the city, and today it is one of the top three reasons why tourists come. Interestingly, club culture has attracted the attention of people associated with the IT startup scene, the fashion industry, film, and real estate development, which hints that it has a connection with Richard Florida's (2002) thesis about the creative class (Coultate 2016). Amsterdam is another case in point, for it has become one of the top nightlife cities in Europe, attracting tourism, creating jobs, and bringing about a lively urban cultural and nightlife scene. The side effects from litter to noise complaints require special measures for nightlife management, which in the case of Amsterdam is vested to a nightlife mayor (*Nachtburgemeester Amsterdam*), formally head of a non-governmental foundation jointly funded by the city government and the nightlife industry (Scruggs 2017). The challenge is obvious: "nurturing the Dutch city's ever-expanding night economy, while satisfying residents and public officials who would sometimes rather it didn't exist." A few other Dutch cities have nightlife mayors, as have a few other larger cities in Europe, such as Toulouse, Zurich, and Paris (Henley 2016).

While personal health, mind-body harmony, nutrition, and exercise are self-evidently part of a holistic personal health project, how about *sexuality*? This last represents the frontier that quickly brings us to pleasures, human desires, and lust, and through them to a host of controversial issues and to negative impacts of hedonistic or imprudent behavior. This leads us to topics that reflect a darker side of the picture, that is, public and community health issues relating to unhealthy lifestyles, as in the case of needing to eliminate tobacco and alcohol abuse, or controlling overmedication or drug use, or to irresponsible lifestyles that are addressed in protection against sexually transmitted diseases and prevention of teenage pregnancies (Edlin et al. 2000).

In spite of such remarks, sexuality is a fundamental human need and a wellness issue in its own right. Safe and enjoyable sex generally has positive impact on personal health. Yet, it is also a social issue in the sense that our *sexual citizenship* shapes our access to resources, recognition, and representation (Klugman 2007), and our ability to live according to our sexual identity or orientation directly affects our subjective well-being. Sexuality is also a sensitive matter and a basic need that is difficult to fully satisfy regardless of social status, age, or gender (see e.g. Morgentaler 2013). This is a particularly difficult problem with disabled people, for whom some liberal European countries have designed sexual assistance services.

Although sexuality is definitively about wellness, for some reason it has been largely silenced in wellness discourse. There are two areas in which *sexual wellness* is visible in contemporary societies, those of medicalization and commercialization of sexuality. With regard to the first, the medical, therapeutic, and educational side of the picture includes hospitals and health care services (e.g. Sexual Health Clinics of Toronto Public Health, Canada), small-scale private specialized clinics and service providers (such as the Rochester Center for Sexual Wellness, Rochester, New York), and non-profit charitable organizations (such as the Compass Center for Sexual Wellness in Edmonton, Alberta, Canada). Added to these are sex-related public health, and devices and products designed to promote safe sex (contraceptives, condoms, etc.).

The other side of sexual wellness, the *sex industry*, is a huge global business, for prostitution alone is worth close to USD 200 billion worldwide. Other goods and services of the industry include pornography, pleasure-enhancing devices, sexual wellness products, sensual pleasure products, distribution channels (e.g. sex shops), and services, including erotic massage parlors, strippers and erotic dancing, telephone and virtual sex, and sex tourism. At the same time the entire industry suffers from serious problems, including crime, drug use, human trafficking and slavery, and sexually transmitted diseases (Ward and Aral 2006). This is evidently the reason why sex in general can have a questionable or negative impact on the image of a city.

In terms of locality development, there are facilities from sex drive-ins, quirky massage parlors, love hotels, and mega-brothels combined with studios, saunas, or dance clubs. Such hot spots can be found in most major cities in the developed world, some of the most luxurious sites being Club LV in Amsterdam, Stuttgart's branch of the Paradise brothel chain in Germany, Sheri's Ranch near Las Vegas, Pink Place in South Melbourne, or Ginza Club in Sydney, Australia, Utopia or La Belle in Bangkok, Thailand, and Café Millennium in São Paulo, Brazil (Starr 2015). Geographical concentrations of the sex industry are called *red-light districts*, such as De Wallen, which is the largest and best known of its kind in Amsterdam, with brothels and sex shops, and undeniably one of the attractions of the city. The promotion of brothels and red-light districts requires decriminalization or legalization of prostitution, as has been done in the Netherlands and Germany. It is a way of reducing the underground economy and providing better tools for government to combat sexual exploitation, improve sex workers' work conditions, and address sex-related health issues at the intersection of public and occupational health.

Sexuality also plays a role in urban tourism, of which there are plenty of examples in Europe—Amsterdam the most prominent. On other continents and cultures, it is worth mentioning Bahrain in the Middle East, Metro Manila in the Philippines, and Rio de Janeiro, São Paulo, and Fortaleza in Brazil. Supply and demand meet in these and many other cities, but as long as this business is part of an underground economy and sex workers work in the informal labor market, or even as sex slaves, "sex tourism" is hardly what city governments want to promote.

It is worth emphasizing that there are also cultural, artistic, and soft-core approaches to sexuality in cultural institutions, museums, and theme parks. There are erotic museums in Amsterdam, Barcelona, Berlin, Paris, Hamburg, and many other Western and Eastern European cities, as well as a few in American and Asian cities. In Jeju Island, South Korea, there is an erotic theme park, Loveland, where hundreds of statues are erected for the pleasure of visitors. In Brazil, there is a plan to build a new sex-themed, adults-only amusement park, Erotika Land, to open in 2018 in the city of Piracicaba, a two-hour drive from São Paulo (Murano 2016). The plan has sparked some debate locally and beyond, as one can guess, and skepticism about the project was crystallized by a council member of Piracicaba: "We can not be known as the capital of sex. That would be bad for our image. In fact, this business could bring prostitution and drug use to the city" (Kemp 2016).

Even in one of the most liberal cities in Europe, Amsterdam, in their rebranding project in the first half of the 2000s, the only theme they wanted to be a less pronounced feature of their city profile was "Sex, Drugs and Rock 'n' Roll." In spite of that, the city has above-average tolerance of the idea that people may be into pornography, prostitution, or even soft drugs. The Netherlands follows a liberal policy, which relies on self-determination and everyone's right to decide about their own health, on the one hand, and on a collective attempt to avoid the negative impacts of the criminalization of prostitution or the use of soft drugs, on the other. A central argument for such an approach is supported by experiences of the prohibition of alcohol during the twentieth century, which have not been particularly encouraging anywhere in the world (e.g. Skelton 2017). Concerning wellness and substance abuse, the avoidance of smoking, alcohol, drugs, or other harmful substances is certainly in line with the idea of holistic wellness, but how such problems should be dealt with is another issue, in which liberalism and conservativism form the two opposing ideological camps.

Many of the wellness issues are ultimately questions of freedom and identity, which makes them complicated and at times controversial. A much-discussed issue in this respect is the freedom of *sexual orientation* and the related rise of *LGBT communities* in liberal countries (lesbian, gay, bisexual, and transgender people). This is a genuine wellness issue, for in a conservative society people with an alternative social or sexual identity may be subject to exclusion, harassment, or even criminal prosecution, which is evidently devastating to their well-being. When measured by LGBT rights, safety, openness, nightlife, and dating, the top ten LGBT cities in the world in 2017 were Madrid, Amsterdam, Toronto, Tel Aviv, London, Berlin, Brighton, Barcelona, New York, and San Francisco (Nestpick.com n/a). "Pink money," or the consumption power of the LGBT community, is economically significant, as are all LGBT-owned businesses or the "rainbow economy," which is slowly becoming part of the mainstream economy, at least in liberal Western economies. Such businesses are often catering for the LGBT community, including tourism, entertainment, hospitality, and consumer goods. This niche has considerable business potential, which implies that supporting LGBT rights is good for the economy (Lee Badget et al. 2014).

Lastly, *naturism* is a matter of well-being, to a degree, at least for those who think that "not wearing clothes is good for body and mind" (Huffman 2015). Naturism or nudism is one of those areas that many consider obscene, upsetting, shameful, or at least extravagant, even if millions of people practice it in one way or another. There have been nudist and clothing-optional beaches for a long time, but now the trend is slowly sneaking into cities. A few cities allow nudity in designated places, one of them being Munich in Germany, which allows nudity in six official "Urban Naked Zones". There are number of nudist resorts in Spain, including Charco del Palo naturist holiday village in Lanzarote in the Canary Islands, and the naturist area north of Vera Playa, Spain, which includes apartment complexes and a hotel that permits naturism. However, the world's largest nude resort town can be found in France. It is Cap d'Agde, a seaside resort on the Mediterranean, which attracts tens of thousands of people in summer, many of whom head there simply because of a chance to be—or to be seen—naked. Some have described its *Village Naturiste*, a family-friendly self-contained town, as "sexual social democracy" served by a fully functioning town, including pools, apartment complexes, a hotel, a bank, a post office, launderettes, hairdressers, supermarkets, nightclubs, and concrete arcades lined with shops and boutiques (Hoad 2015). Urban naked zones, naturist communities and resorts, and nudist beaches may not become mainstream globally in the near future, but for some liberal cities and resort towns, they open up opportunities for benefiting from such a niche tourism.

In terms of business potential, urban consumption, entertainment, party and nightlife culture, and the varieties of the expressions of freedom and human desire are an essential part of local economic development. Even if identity issues, controversies, and externalities characterize this area of wellness, local communities benefit from co-ordinated promotion of wellness-oriented hospitality and retail businesses, health entertainment, urban cultural attractions, and lifestyle niche economies, most notably nude and rainbow economies.

Environmental Wellness

Nature or the totality of the elements of the natural world is an inherent aspect of human wellness. It is not only a fundamental setting of life containing both life-bringing and destructive forces, but it is also our most natural habitat with a restorative effect. In various forms and in varying degrees it has the potential to heal us, ease our pain, and improve our health. This is why the human–nature connection is a fundamental nexus of wellness. A concept that cherishes that idea is ecological or environmental wellness or *EcoWellness*, which sees sustainability and human well-being as interconnected phenomena (Bandarage 2013). EcoWellness comprises three discrete dimensions: (1) access to nature; (2) environmental identity; and (3) transcendence in nature. There are good or positive environments that enhance well-being and contribute to health, whereas negative environments, such as the inner-city housing without any access to nature, distract from health and contribute to non-healthy responses to life. Interestingly, the process by which wellness can be harnessed through access to nature seems to be closely related to how a person identifies with the environment or how he or she incorporates nature into the conception of self. Transcendence refers to feelings of interconnectedness and unity with all things, which boils down to the two aspects of spirituality and community connectedness (Reese and Myers 2012). The ultimate need for EcoWellness is obvious in contemporary urban life characterized by increased penetration of ubiquitous technologies, high urban density, and social alienation (Louv 2014).

Many of the natural assets available to an urban community are vital for wellness development, including the sea, rivers, lakes, springs, shores, mountains, forests, plants, natural sounds, clean air, open sky, and climatic features. Their tamed forms include parks, vertical gardens, and green roofs. Urban nature, even if "domesticated" to a degree, is an important part of balanced development. In many cities, there are attempts at ecological conservation, safeguarding urban species and restoring their habitats, and increasing local inhabitants' connection with nature, as in the case of the Nature in the City program in Fort Collins, Colorado, and in San Francisco, California, in the USA. Urban agriculture or vertical farming is another emerging trend, which has become a notable trend in cities like New York and Chicago (Scipioni 2016).

Nature has a significant public and economic value. *Parks, forests, and green spaces* have direct use value, environmental benefits, and an impact on health, and they also affect the valuation of adjacent properties (Wolf 2004). Its role in local economic development can be direct or indirect, as in the appeal of natural attractions and wonders, or in the utilization of nature as a factor in production, or as a kind of facilitative environment. Nature is also self-evidently an essential element in the beautification and aestheticization of the city.

A core dimension of the essence of the city as a high-density settlement is the *built environment*. What makes such an environment so important is that people's experiences of places are central to their well-being, their physical health, their communal and social lives, and their identities. Understanding this relationship provides an incentive to rethink urban planning and especially to create better-designed and healthier environments that meet basic human and social needs (Goldhagen 2017). In *The Well-Tempered City*, Jonathan F. P. Rose distills his interdisciplinary research and firsthand experience into a model for how to design and reshape cities with the goal of equalizing their landscape of opportunity. He borrows the concept of "temperament" from music to describe a way of achieving harmony. He argues that *well-tempered cities* can be infused with systems that bend the arc of their development towards coherence, equality, resilience, circularity, adaptability, well-being, compassion, and the ever-unfolding harmony between civilization and nature (Rose 2016).

Even if physical structures are the most concrete and visible elements of a city, it is what they are used for that makes the city, which emphasizes the role of logistics, functionalities, utilities, and services. A wealthy city that offers sufficient natural-physical amenities, pleasant (gentrified) residential areas, and good services, lively retail markets, and leisure and cultural amenities, can be called a ***high amenity city*** (cf. Greene 2006). In its paradigmatic form, it is a middle-sized city surrounded by a scenic natural environment, devoid of urban sprawl and overcrowding. It is usually well planned, blessed by a thriving historic central business district, well connected to regional retail centers—possibly designed as attractive lifestyle centers—and housing subdivisions designed with sustainability in mind. Examples of such cities include Portland, Oregon, Boulder, Colorado, and Santa Fe, New Mexico (Thrall 2002).

High-amenity cities lead us to ***livability***, which is not only good for residents but has a particular value in place promotion and branding. It has also a kind of facilitative role in urban wellness. Livability is inherently associated with a city that gives well-being, health, and cultural experiences a role in its development policy. It is peculiar that in global urban livability rankings it is usually middle-sized or large cities in affluent European or White Commonwealth countries (e.g. Vienna, Zurich, Copenhagen, Toronto), with a relatively low population density, that get the best scores, measured by indicators of personal freedom, quality of life, cultural assets, basic services, health, safety, and environment (Anttiroiko 2014a).

In terms of economic development policy, livability is assumed to attract demand and visitors, serve the local economy, and indirectly even contribute to generating exports in services. It serves the wellness of local residents, which is important. However, its true power lies in its ability to attract visitors to enjoy the city. The next question is how to "productize" or wrap all this up to make it useful for city marketing. We can approach this as a destination management or town center management issue. Concerning the former, the attraction by livability and related urban amenities can be improved by utilizing the following kinds of factors:

- urban beaches and waterfront areas
- pleasant, safe streets and good cycling routes
- gardens and parks
- architecture and urban design
- infrastructure, transport, and housing
- recycling, cleanliness, and safety.

Creating an attractive and livable city requires ***place shaping***, which describes the ways in which local players collectively use their influence, powers, creativity, and abilities to create attractive, prosperous, and safe communities, which attract tourists and where people want to live, work, and do business. A fundamental principle underpinning place shaping is the idea that every place should have an identity, a function, and an economic purpose. In local economic development this requires that discussion about "place" is explicitly connected with discussions about a city's economic profile. In England, for example, local authorities and businesses have set new Local Enterprise Partnerships to help determine local economic priorities and lead economic growth and job creation within the local area and to integrate economic development with a range of other functions. The same tendency can be seen in town center management (Coca-Stefaniak et al. 2009). A smaller-scale development with an explicit connection to the place and business is known as a business improvement district, which secures private capital for improving the attractiveness of a city's central areas (Meltzer 2012) and to enhance sales growth and increase property values (Ha and Grunwell 2014). These aspects of locality development relate to wellness real estate.

It is easy to pinpoint the general relevance of natural assets, built environments, and urban dynamism and livability in wellness-oriented urban economic development. The key point here is the crucial role both nature and built environment play in securing wellness at community level. The other important element is livability and overall attractiveness, which is crucial to wellness destinations, retail businesses, and property owners.

Medicine, Science, and Technology

We can start the discussion about wellness-related science and technology with a modern hospital, for it is evidently a center of research-based and technologically driven health care. As mentioned earlier, wellness together with modern medicine can be called Wellness+. The further extension of this scheme is life sciences, the pharmaceutical industry, and wellness and medical technologies. Thus, "soft" wellness (spa) and "hard" wellness (medicine) together with a wide spectrum from life sciences to health technologies can be referred to as Wellness++.

Life sciences describe a wide range of sciences that relate to the study of living organisms, including ecology, biology and other biosciences, genetics, anatomy, physiology, neuroscience, environmental health, food science, nutrition, pharmaceutical sciences, and many others. One of its core areas is health science or *medicine*, which as an applied science focuses on the diagnosis, treatment, and prevention of diseases. Life sciences contribute to health and wellness in various ways through applications in health care, devices, drugs, and nutrition. Life sciences, medicine, biotechnology, and pharmaceutical sciences have their equivalents in industry, making them a genuine global mega-industry at the intersection of science, technology, and health. They have become particularly visible at local level in health districts and health care hubs that connect hospitals and health care institutions with surrounding communities, as well as in medical, biotech, and biopharma clusters, and industrial districts. There are hundreds of science parks and local or regional clusters with life sciences, medicine, or biotech as their industrial priority.

Wellness and technology is a chapter of its own in the book of Wellness++. New opportunities provided by wellness technology businesses emerge from the need to reverse the current state of chronic diseases with the support of new centers of technologically driven wellness that go beyond the hospital. An underlying idea is that they should facilitate us at the moment when we make choices in daily life that affect our wellness (Teshler 2016). *Wellness technology* itself has advanced far beyond mere temperature readings and now make it possible to control, track, measure, and monitor body functions and actions. We can receive real-time feedback that helps us make informed decisions about our food intake, sun exposure, or stress level. We may also vacation or live in smart dwellings designed to assist us in realizing our quest for healthy living (Harding-Bond 2017).

There is a wide range of devices, wearables, mobile apps for wellness, and smart micro-environments, which cover all aspects of human life, including happiness, meditation, healthy emotions, healthy eating, weight loss, fitness, brain power, better sleep, stress relief, and overall health (Valdez 2016; Cattel and Watson 2016). Let us take a quick glance at some of them.

Special wellness condominiums and single-family homes have been built in different parts of the USA, some of them offer close to 100 wellness features. The same trend is spreading slowly to the hotel business. The world's first wellness hotel rooms saw the light of day in the MGM Grand Hotel & Casino in Las Vegas. So-called, Stay Well rooms include such amenities as a vitamin C infused shower, dawn simulation, air purification system, cedar closets, aromatherapy, energizing light, and many more. Similarly, there is a smart kitchen concept in the making that enhances traditional meal preparation and cooking processes by raising awareness of nutrition facts about food.

Another category is *technological devices, accessories, and sensing applications*, which are used for medical, fitness, and control functions. For example: sensor-loaded athletic apparel can monitor progress on a mobile device; moisture-wicking gear that uses a Siri-style assistant to record and inform in real time on oxygen intake during workouts; gear that measures sleep quality; and a onesie type outfit for children that is able to track sleep status, breathing, and body position while allowing parents to listen in (Harding-Bond 2017).

One of the most quickly developing fields of wellness technologies is *wearables*. Some activity trackers and personal training monitors originated in the 1980s and 1990s, but wellness wearables started to mushroom in the 2010s. Although awareness of wearable technology—from fitness bands for self-monitoring to mobile health devices for tracking and monitoring medical conditions—is high among consumers in developed countries, most notably in the USA, few are actually using them so far. However, their use has steadily increased in both medical care and wellness (Harding-Bond 2017). *Smart wearables and handheld devices* are often used as platforms for measuring personal activity through sensors and mobile applications, including socks with sensors, a smart watch application for safety and other functions, smart pill bottles, playful toothbrushes for kids, health-tracking briefs, wearable underwear that detects falls, smart footwear, a persuasive robotic assistant for health self-management of senior citizens, a smart thermometer, and customized mental health help known as ThriveOn. Already millions of Americans are using a fitness and health app with their smartphones, and the trend is likely to spread throughout the world.

Web^2 (Web squared), IoT, gamification, and mobile applications are reshaping traditional wellness programs. Most notably, *persuasive technologies* can be leveraged to create engaging, motivating, and impactful wellness programs at individual, group, and collective levels (Orji and Moffatt 2016). According to Nielsen's health and wellness survey, more than 70% of Americans say they are actively working to become healthier or maintain their current health. Despite such responses, few are engaging with the digital realm to help reach their health goals (Nielsen 2014). Indeed, it is not self-evident that such applications are always positively received by customers, or that they bring sufficient added value on all occasions (e.g. Kaye 2017). In any case, an important additional feature that is likely to change this picture is the increased connectedness of wellness devices and wearables with social media, which provides new opportunities for wellness-oriented social interaction, social networking, and the enhancement of health informatics (Munson et al. 2010; Young 2010).

The adoption of new wellness devices and services by a sufficiently large segment of consumers has led to the rise of new businesses and start-ups that target these growing markets; at the same time, many existing companies are expanding their offerings to retain their customers and meet the needs of tech-savvy users. A critical factor of such a technology-based field is that available services are heavily tied to the underlying technologies and platforms, be it smartphone, a computer system, or a broader IT ecosystem (Annanperä 2017). Such a conditioning factor increases systemic interdependence and platform-dependency, which creates both opportunities and threats for both wellness businesses and local developers.

What is the relevance of Wellness++ in terms of business potential? First and foremost, science and technology are tightly connected with health and wellness, and are likely to cause dramatic changes in the near future in both wellness-oriented consumption and production. Science and technology are actually pervasively connected with almost anything that relates to human health and well-being. Technological development is a kind of framing megatrend that will affect wellness demand and supply, not only through technological devices but also through connectedness, virtualization, and platformization. In all, at the intersection of scientific research, technological innovations, life sciences and related industries, health care systems, and "softer" areas of holistic wellness, Wellness++ forms a high value-added global mega industry with promising prospects for local economic growth for those cities that meet the technological, scientific, and educational requirements of such a knowledge-based development.

Intellectual Wellness

Intellectuality as a broad category includes intellectual life, education, critical thinking, professional competence, and self-development. It has a connection with occupational wellness, including such themes as career and work and, through them, as a rather distant dimension, economic or financial wellness.

At the personal level, *intellectual wellness* is about having a mind open to new ideas (Edlin et al. 2000). It refers to an ability to acquire knowledge and understanding, and to learn from previous experiences that are needed to manage everyday and professional lives and to make smart and mature judgments in given situations. In its most advanced forms intellectuality refers to personal growth, that is, to mental and spiritual development through which we become wiser and better people.

Intellectuality has reflections at different levels of urban life. Actually, it relates to one of the core functions of cities, as they are centers of knowledge, learning, and innovation. Such features of the city are essential when considering how people strive for higher intellectuality and personal growth. This is a particular area where a demarcation between knowledge, innovation, or a learning city and a wellness city is worth pondering. This does not only have to be taken as a theoretical issue, but also as a practical question of what aspects of urban knowledge processes, institutions, networks, and outputs relate to wellness. The rule of thumb here is that those aspects of intellectuality, knowledge, and learning that support holistic views of health, community-level wellness, wellness-focused businesses, and global knowledge processes associated with wellness, form a part of wellness discourse. Such wellness-related knowledge processes have two basic modes: *global knowledge processes* are most critical in wellness high-tech and medical fields, and large spa, beauty, and fitness destinations, and in wellness real estate (cf. Bathelt et al. 2004); while *local knowledge processes* are based on local wisdom, traditions, and authentic people encompassing such wellness areas as local food culture, healing traditions, local spiritual sites, local lifestyles, and local cultural events (cf. Polanyi 1967; Berman 2017).

Previous discussion urges us to pay special attention to three interrelated issues: knowledge base of community wellness; wellness-focused education, research, and R&D; and educational and intellectual aspects of occupational wellness. Let us focus next on the topic that is at the heart of the idea of a wellness city, that of wellness-oriented informatics, community capacity, and local knowledge institutions.

Community wellness represents an approach that strives to balance the promotion of individual wellness with the collective goals of the community. Communities promote individual wellness by supporting the factors that enhance it, improving health awareness, and providing local conditions for healthy living. Moos (2003) describes three broad areas that enhance well-being and increase social and performance outcomes: strength of social ties; directions of personal growth; and supportive structures provided by the environment. A combined focus on these three factors is essential as none of them in isolation can ensure wellness (Schueller 2009).

Societal structures and institutions relating to human rights, democracy, and equality covary with levels of subjective well-being. Furthermore, communities can promote positive relationships by supporting individual diversity and fostering group cohesion. In this way, communities high in wellness provide the resources and opportunities necessary for individuals to form connections and develop skills needed to improve *social capital* (Schueller 2009). Such efforts maximize a community's capacity for *positivity* by developing and enhancing the strengths of individual community members and focusing on building group cohesion through meaning and purpose. *Community capacity* for positivity is the local collective ability to enhance positive emotions, engagement, meaning, and purpose in the members of the community. Enhancing community capacity towards positivity reflects Abraham Maslow's notion that societies or cultures can be either growth-promoting or growth-inhibiting. Growth-promoting communities utilize individual and community strengths (Schueller 2009). This implies, in real life, a courage to identify, openly discuss, and intervene in the inhibiting factors, of which illuminating examples are bullying at schools or in workplaces (Migliaccio and Raskauskas 2016) and social exclusion and alienation in community life.

Collective action that empowers and motivates individuals to make healthy choices will improve the health of communities and contribute to community development. One particular way of facilitating such developments is to establish *community knowledge centers* (CKCs), which can be publicly or privately funded, or be a partnership-based endeavor. Such centers allow both public and charitable organizations and other members of the community to spread the word about the work they do for the community. They have a particular role in providing access for disadvantaged groups and communities to global knowledge through information and communication technology (ICT). The CKC in Toronto, for example, connects philanthropy with community needs and opportunities by bringing people together to share their stories, showcase their trials and achievements, and engage residents in discovering the powerful impact they can make in supporting innovative solutions to some of the city's most pressing issues. Such community knowledge process facilitation has a connection with the use of crowdsourcing, living labs, and participatory innovation platforms (Anttiroiko 2016). There are also integrated centers that bring learning and wellness under the same roof in the name of community well-being. A case in point is the Dahlia Campus for Health and

Well-Being, which was set up in early 2016 in one of Denver's poorest neighborhoods (PBS 2017).

In countries where *libraries* have a long history and prestigious position as local knowledge and entertainment hubs, public libraries have assumed a critical role in community development (Anttiroiko and Savolainen 2007). Larger libraries can even play an important role in providing materials and services to the local business community (Glass et al. 2000). More importantly, libraries serve the wider community as a hub of entertainment, culture, and learning, and thus contribute to community well-being, and indirectly to local economic development (Hamilton-Pennell 2008).

A knowledge institution par excellence is a *university*, which has an interesting role to play in urban wellness. Education itself has a close connection with health, and through health informatics and learning affects community wellness (Callejo Perez and Ode 2013). It is further claimed that universities are replacing banks and corporate offices as the driving forces behind urban development, and one of the core expertise areas that enhances such development is health. It is as if universities together with health institutions contribute to pulling employment, resources, and knowledge back to city centers and urban campuses. For example, in downtown Atlanta high-rise banks and company headquarters are rivaled by Emory University Hospital, with several independent clinics inside the hospital and the Centers for Disease Control and Prevention in midtown. Moreover, in many cities new developments include life-science or health care technology centers, health research facilities, and teaching hospitals, many of them funded fully or partly privately, making them among the most dynamic forces to attract capital, knowledge, and people to city centers throughout the developed world during last few decades (Blankenhorn 2010).

Last but not least, the post-war decades witnessed the emergence of a new discourse on the connection between universities and the economy, addressing the ways of turning science into business (e.g. Kotha et al. 2014), the role of higher education institutions in economic life (Lester 2005; see also Pillay 2011), the emergence of academic capitalism and entrepreneurial universities (Anttiroiko 2014b), and relationships between universities, government, and business, known as the Triple Helix (Etzkowitz and Leydesdorff 2000). A model that takes this discussion further in terms of citizen and community involvement is the *Quadruple Helix innovation theory* (Monteiro and Carayannis 2017). It provides a synthesis of top-down policies and practices from government, university, and industry, balanced and shaped by bottom-up initiatives and actions by civil society. This approach highlights the creation of differentiated productive units that interact with and complement each other in the production of continuous innovation and the management of their connections as the precondition for economic growth. This leads us to the role of intellectuality, learning, and personal growth in the context of wellness, not through the lenses of special groups targeted in attraction policies but rather as the factors of production and the sources of innovation and endogenous local growth. This entails that actors of civil society are not seen only as users or customers that help firms to create better product innovations, but as people with a multiplicity of roles, such as inhabitants of urban neighborhoods, civic activists, local entrepreneurs and experts, ethnic minorities, and the representatives of special socio-economic demographics and age groups living in the community, who can contribute in various ways to community development, urban regeneration, and local innovation processes.

To sum up, what is the general relevance of intellectuality, learning, and personal growth in terms of business potential within a wellness city framework? A strategic area worth a closer look is wellness-related knowledge processes, which can contribute to publishing, media, education, research, and urban development. There are, for example, wellness academies and training organizations, which turn knowledge into business as well as degree programs in wellness, such as the Degree Program in Experience and Wellness Management (EXWEL) in Haaga-Helia University of Applied Sciences in Helsinki, Finland. Another form in which knowledge relates to wellness-oriented location development is the creation of knowledge centers and participatory platforms, which are used to facilitate wellness-focused community informatics, open and user innovation, and product development. In all, the way intellectuality relates to wellness is mainly through its facilitative role in supporting urban communities' health informatics, and knowledge and innovation processes.

Social and Cultural Wellness

Human well-being is not only a matter of narrowly defined personal health, but also the well-being of a human as a social creature, who determines his/her identity through social interaction, who needs other people in order to live a full life, and who creates, shares, applies, and transmits cultural values and practices. In short, we become human beings in the socio-cultural environment.

Holistic well-being has a social and cultural dimension, which relates to identity, belonging, and cultural experiences. *Social wellness* is about healthy social relations and identity, while *cultural wellness* is based on our experiences of a rich cultural environment. The cultural side of wellness has a connection to different forms of art—experiencing the magic of paintings or listening to music—and cultural amenities such as museums, art exhibitions, concerts, movies, local literature, dance, and cultural festivals. These two dimensions mingle in our positive feelings for a diversity of cultures and an ability to interact with all kinds of people, irrespective of their ethnicity, religion, language, class, gender, or age. From the point of view of locality development, such a socio-cultural dimension of wellness relies on locally rooted, authentic elements of local history and culture.

From the point of view of wellness, our experiences of people, places, and events affect our well-being. For instance, visiting Mozart's Salzburg or Vienna can add an essential flavor to the well-being of a dedicated fan of classical music, and walking through the Brontës' moors in Haworth, West Yorkshire, may be a delightful experience if the person in question happens to be fascinated by the literature and culture of nineteenth-century England. The same goes with visiting film locations, birth places of famous people, or natural and architectural wonders of the world, such as cultural heritage sites defined by UNESCO. Such features give cities special advantages, as evidenced by such European cultural and historical cities as, for example, Venice, Florence, Vienna, Athens, Rome, Paris, and London. A good example of a city that benefits local culture in its economic development policy is Kanazawa in Japan, a UNESCO Creative City of Crafts and Folk Art, which utilizes in its creative city policy its industrial history, old city districts, handcraft, cuisine, performing arts, literature, museums, and natural assets. A special challenge for culturally oriented location development is an inevitable tension between the authenticity of cultural amenities and pervasive commercialization (Kloosterman 2014).

Socio-cultural wellness manifests itself in various places and situations. *Home* as a permanent place of residence is vital for wellness, as it affects significantly the conditions of our lives. With respect to economic development, it forms a *home-oriented leisure cluster*, including household and kitchen appliances, cookware, home decoration, and gardening (Kotro et al. 2005). The other vital place is *work*, within which employers promote workplace wellness (Gatchel and Schultz 2012). In urban life, sociability, play, and adventure become particularly visible in "third places" of the city, that is, places where we spend time while not at home (first place) or at work (second place), referring to places like cafés, clubs, libraries, and parks. They are places that bring people together and make cities attractive. As sites of interaction, they are also significant for the fundamental elements of social life, such as civic activism, democratic practices, and activities that contribute to identity building (Oldenburg 1989). Lastly, new trends in wellness sometimes blur the boundaries of these places, for public spaces are often used as extended living rooms and as outdoor office spaces or "gyms," such as *boot camp* sessions in the local park.

Wellness-related socio-cultural activities that usually take place in third places include social interaction, play, and adventure, sometimes referred to as *creative leisure* (Benkö et al. 2017). Humans are inherently playful and this play is an important element in culture. Sure, all mammals play, but no other species pursues such a wide variety of entertainment, plays with words, or uses their imagination in the process the way humans do (Holmes and Douglas 2012). It is not a surprise that a special form of a third place are *sites of play*, such as playgrounds distributed in different parts of the city. Commercially significant sites of play include theme parks, amusement parks, sites of "edutainment," such as science museums, and, as one of the latecomers, augmented reality and the gamification of the city, such as the location-based augmented reality game Pokémon Go launched in 2016.

From an economic point of view, *amusement and theme parks* have had a special place in the scene of cultural wellness for a long time. They include everything from the Walt Disney World resort complex in Florida to smaller theme parks around the world. Beside these, there are places like Children's City in Dubai, an educational city devoted to children where they can investigate, explore, play, discover, and learn about the world we live in. Another example is the chain of Legoland theme parks, the first of its kind set up by Lego in Billund, Denmark.

Entertainment, sociability, and play have also found their way to cities through *fairs, carnivals, festivals, and other events*. Terms such as festivalization and eventification have emerged to describe this phenomenon and its rising importance in urban development, which provides shared interests for local stakeholders, producers, and marketers of cultural products, and new opportunities for players in the experience economy to be integrated into urban growth coalitions (Jacob 2012). Wellness has become part of that trend. Thousands of wellness, lifestyle, healthy food, fitness, and sports *festivals* are organized on a yearly basis, especially in the USA and Europe (Raphael 2017). Wellness that has found an urban home in day spas and fitness clubs is gaining increased visibility in urban public spaces and learning a new way of consuming the city itself.

What is the general relevance of culture and sociability in location development within a wellness city framework? First, historical sites and cultural amenities are essential for the richness and depth of life. They are self-evidently fundamental elements of urban wellness. Another key area are the sites of joy and play, ranging from cafés and other public places to dedicated sites such as theme parks. The third element is eventification and the increased interest in wellness festivals. Both sites of play and events increase urban livability and, for the same reason, contribute to building an image of a socially and culturally attractive city.

Spiritual Wellness

This category relates to such themes as happiness, mental balance, stress management, mindfulness, meditation, personal growth, self-actualization, spirituality, and transcendence. At an individual level, we can speak about personal feelings, happiness, state of mind, emotional wellness, emotional intelligence, and spiritual strength. At community level, these aspects of life become institutionalized, as in the cases of retreats, meditation centers, or churches. At the highest level of abstraction, we can speak of the transcendental dimension of human life, which takes us to spirituality and such concepts as divinity and immortality.

Spirituality is a widely recognized element of human well-being, usually described as the "third element" of the body–mind–soul triangle. It has both personal and community dimensions, the latter creating a natural connection with urban development. Spirituality as a community-level phenomenon has a connection to community welfare. Active local associations, tolerant religious communities, sports clubs, and civic groups are essential for tackling a range of social, economic, and political challenges, from crime to sustainability to the provision of care. Giving them a role in local development means that the local community as a whole is taken into the heart of policy making (Taylor 2011). Spirituality, mindfulness, and self-actualization have inspired several destinations, which form a part of wellness-oriented local development, including:

- Meditation retreats, yoga centers, and silent stay retreats
- Mindfulness spas and spa hotels
- Churches, monasteries, Buddhist temples, places of worship, and spiritual retreats
- Special holy sites and holy cities
- Pilgrimage destinations, memorial sites, and cemeteries.

Many of these sites are retreats located outside urban centers. There are, however, some areas in which cities have their own role, for instance as cities of churches, the most famous example being Rome. *Churches* are institutions that form a part of local economy. Churches and other houses of worship hire workers, make investments, and maintain premises, and some progressive churches offer various ancillary services, such as childcare, senior citizen housing, drug abuse treatment programs, and educational and cultural services (Reed 1994). Participants in religious organizations represent a significant market for religious goods and services, including publishing, inspirational merchandise, and audio, video, and software products. Churches may also contribute directly to economic development by taking an active role in improving the economic status of the communities in which they interact (Hamilton-Pennell 2009). One strategy is to start the economic empowerment from church members who then further empower their surrounding neighborhoods. In multicultural areas, this support may be directed to providing support or services to special target groups, such as disadvantaged groups, ethnic minorities, or women-owned businesses (Jacobs 2009).

The impact of religiosity on economic performance and vice versa is one of the fundamental issues relating to the relationship between spirituality and economy (Barro and McCleary 2003). What is of special interest in this book are local destinations at the intersection of locality, spirituality, and economy. A case in point is religious or secular pilgrimage as a special form of wellness tourism. A *pilgrimage* refers to a journey to places of religious or spiritual importance. Meeting such a spiritual quest has an external dimension, as in visiting holy sites, as well as an internal dimension relating to spiritual experience and internal understanding. What is new in this picture is the surge of secular journeys that resemble traditional, religiously motivated, pilgrimages (Collins-Kreiner 2010).

Pilgrimage is sometimes as similar to "existential tourism," in its faith, symbolism, and authenticity. To conceptualize this, Cohen (1992) identified five primary modes of the tourist experience based on the place and significance of the given experience in the total world-view of the tourist (Collins-Kreiner 2010). Beside *recreational* and *diversionary* modes of tourism, there are three higher levels of experience sought by tourists. An *experiential* mode of tourism is about a quest for the vicarious experiences of the authentic lifestyle of authentic communities or cultures; *experimental* mode is about trying out various lifestyles that the person could consider adopting for himself or herself; lastly, in the *existential* mode the tourist commits himself to an alternative that becomes for him a new, "elective" center, resembling an idealized pilgrim (Cohen 1992).

Christian pilgrimages to the Holy Land in historical Palestine, the location of events from the Old and New Testaments, together with the religious significance of Jerusalem, makes that area globally unique. However, long-lasting unrest in the area has limited its popularity as a tourist destination, even though its overall appeal, especially among Christians and Jews around the world, is of a lasting nature. Other important sites in the history of spirituality include Rome and many others associated with the apostles, saints, and martyrs. Of course, pilgrimage is also part of other religions, from Judaism to Buddhism, Hinduism, and Islam (see Coleman and Eade 2004). In today's world, famous pilgrimage cities include Fatima in Portugal, Camino de Santiago in Northern Spain, Lourdes in France, and Assisi in Italy—all attracting millions of tourists every year. Some individual religious destinations do much the same, such as the Meiji Shrine in Tokyo, Kiyomizu-dera and Kinkaku-ji temples in Kyoto, Po Lin Monastery and Tian Tan Buddha in Hong Kong, St. Peter's Basilica and Sistine Chapel in the Vatican City inside Rome, St. Mark's Basilica in Venice, Basilica de Sagrada Familia in Barcelona, Notre Dame Cathedral and Sacré Coeur Basilica in Paris, St. Paul's Cathedral in London, and St. Patrick's Cathedral in New York City (Orcutt 2012).

Lastly, the category of *transcendence* brings into the picture a final harbor or ultimate mystery of self-actualization. It takes us to the perception of death as well as to the mystery of what happens to us after we die. From our point of view, the question is not that much about the afterlife but about how our perception of such fundamental issues affects our well-being while still alive. This relates in a complicated way to treatment for a terminal illness, hospices, suicide, euthanasia, and funerals. What is special in treating the terminally ill is their need for both palliative and compassionate care. Much the same can be said about euthanasia. All such issues go beyond personal health, for they have deep roots and a resonance in the philosophy of life, ethics, social order, and public policy. This area includes difficult topics, such as *suicide*, which is a taboo in wellness discourse. Suffice to say here that suicide as a personal solution to end one's life can be seen as an expression of a total lack of wellness. There are famous suicide spots in different parts of the world, such as Aokigahara forest in Japan, which are manifestations of mythology, existential and social crises, and probably public policy failures as well. Such places may occasionally become sites of *dark tourism*. Even if dark tourism as a whole exerts its appeal to death, suffering, horror, and disaster—its attractions range from themed museums to real sites of tragedy—and thus represents everything wellness discourse wants to avoid for understandable reasons, motives for visiting such places are often educational and emotional, relating to healing, heritage, identity, and commemoration (see Lennon and Foley 2006). This is why even dark tourism may occasionally have a connection with real-life wellness.

While the fate of our soul after death may remain mystery, at least we know that it is a custom to arrange funerals; bodies—or cremated remains placed in an urn—are buried in cemeteries or other memorial sites, and afterwards people may visit our grave. Religious institutions have their essential role in both funerals and cemeteries, but the latter are, at the same time, unconventional businesses. *Cemeteries*, those silent destinations of transcendent wellness, are of particular interest in terms of locality development. People do not necessarily go to cemeteries to cheer up, but such visits do help us become aware of our mortality, build a bigger framework for assessing our hardships, contribute to our striving for a balanced life, and may affect the reprioritization of our goals and values (see The Telegraph 2012).

Many cemeteries attract thousands of visitors a year, sometimes being surprisingly popular destinations. While they are places where people are buried, they are at the same time glimpses of history and places of commemoration, beauty and fragility of life, and tranquility. There are even guided cemetery walks, even though most such visits are self-organized. Examples of famous final resting places are *Cimetière Du Père-Lachaise* in Paris, hosting world-famous artists like Jim Morrison, Oscar Wilde, Edith Piaf, Maria Callas, and Frédéric Chopin; Vienna Central Cemetery (*Wiener Zentralfriedhof*) in Austria, a resting place for many renowned classical composers, such as Ludwig van Beethoven and Franz Schubert; the reputedly haunted Greyfriars Kirkyard in Edinburgh, Scotland, surrounding an old local church at the edge of the old town with hundreds of seventeenth-century graves; Highgate Cemetery in London, UK, with the grave of

Karl Marx, which makes it a primary commemorative site for left-wing sympathizers; and Arlington National Cemetery in the USA, a final resting place of President John F. Kennedy, accompanied by more than 400,000 US soldiers, one of the most patriotic places in the country (see e.g. Minford 2016).

The general relevance of spirituality in terms of wellness business potential lies in the attractiveness and popularity of spiritual destinations, pilgrimages, and famous cemeteries. It may not be that lucrative a business, but it does form part of the urban wellness economy.

References

Andreff, W. (2008). Globalization of the Sports Economy. *Rivista di Diritto ed Economia dello Sport, 4*(3), 13–32.

Annanperä, E. (2017). *Managing Technology-Based Service Innovations in Emerging Wellness Business Ecosystems* (Doctoral Dissertation). Oulu: University of Oulu. Retrieved August 22, 2017, from http://jultika.oulu.fi/files/isbn9789526215839.pdf

Anttiroiko, A.-V. (2014a). *The Political Economy of City Branding*. London/New York: Routledge.

Anttiroiko, A.-V. (2014b). Entrepreneurial Universities in Global Innovation Ecology. In Y. Cai & V. Kohtamäki (Eds.), *Transformation of Higher Education in Innovation Systems in China and Finland* (pp. 37–57). Tampere: Tampere University Press.

Anttiroiko, A.-V. (2016). City-as-a-Platform: The Rise of Participatory Innovation Platforms in Finnish Cities. *Sustainability, 8*(9), Article 922.

Anttiroiko, A.-V., & Savolainen, R. (2007). New Premises of Public Library Strategies in the Age of Globalization. In E. D. Garten, D. E. Williams, J. M. Nyce, & S. Talja (Eds.), *Advances in Library Administration and Organization* (Vol. 25, pp. 61–81). Amsterdam: Elsevier.

APHA. (2017). *What Is Public Health?* Washington, DC: American Public Health Association. Retrieved August 20, 2017, from https://www.apha.org/what-is-public-health

Asch, D. A., & Volpp, K. G. (2012). What Business Are We in? The Emergence of Health as the Business of Health Care. *The New England Journal of Medicine, 367*, 888–889.

Baggott, R. (2011). *Public Health: Politics and Policy* (2nd ed.). Basingstoke: Palgrave Macmillan.

Bandarage, A. (2013). *Sustainability and Well-being: The Middle Path to Environment, Society and the Economy*. Basingstoke: Palgrave Macmillan.

Barro, R., & McCleary, R. (2003). Religion and Economic Growth. *American Sociological Review, 68*(5), 760–781.

Bathelt, H., Malmberg, A., & Maskell, P. (2004). Clusters and Knowledge: Local Buzz, Global Pipelines and the Process of Knowledge Creation. *Progress in Human Geography, 28*(1), 31–56.

Benkö, Z. Z., Modi, I., & Tarkó, K. (Eds.). (2017). *Leisure, Health and Well-Being: A Holistic Approach*. Cham: Springer/Palgrave Macmillan.

Berman, T. (2017). *Public Participation as a Tool for Integrating Local Knowledge into Spatial Planning: Planning, Participation, and Knowledge*. Cham: Springer.

Blakely, E. J., & Bradshaw, T. K. (2002). *Planning Local Economic Development: Theory and Practice* (3rd ed.). Thousand Oaks: Sage.

Blankenhorn, D. (2010, September 22). The Wellness Research Center Boom. *DZNet*. Retrieved September 17, 2017, from http://www.zdnet.com/article/the-wellness-research-center-boom/

Brown, A. (2017, September 23). Do You Know What a Spa Is? *TripSavvy*. Retrieved October 31, 2017, from https://www.tripsavvy.com/what-is-a-spa-3085921

BusinessJyväskylä. (n/a). *Exercise and Well-Being* (Website). Retrieved September 17, 2017, from http://www.businessjyvaskyla.fi/en/fields/wellbeing

Callejo Pérez, D. M., & Ode, J. (Eds.). (2013). *The Stewardship of Higher Education: Re-imagining the Role of Education and Wellness on Community Impact*. Rotterdam: Sense Publishers.

Cattel, J., & Watson, Z. (2016, April 19). The 38 Best Health and Fitness Apps. *Greatist*. Retrieved August 22, 2017, from https://greatist.com/fitness/best-health-fitness-apps

Clark, C. C. (Ed.). (2002). *Health Promotion in Communities: Holistic and Wellness Approaches*. New York: Springer Publishing Company.

Clark, T. N. (Ed.). (2011). *The City as an Entertainment Machine*. Lanham: Lexington Books.

Coca-Stefaniak, J. A., Parker, C., Quin, S., Rinaldi, R., & Byrom, J. (2009). Town Centre Management Models: A European Perspective. *Cities, 26*(2), 74–80.

Cohen, E. (1992). Pilgrimage and Tourism: Convergence and Divergence. In A. Morinis (Ed.), *Sacred Journeys: The Anthropology of Pilgrimage* (pp. 47–61). Westport: Greenwood Press.

Cohen, S. (2016, September 16). 21st-Century Sports: How Digital Technology Is Changing the Face of the Sporting Industry. *The Huffington Post, The Blog*. Retrieved September 17, 2017, from http://www.huffingtonpost.com/sam-cohen/21st-century-sports-how-d_b_12039220.html

Cohen, M., & Bodeker, G. (2008). *Understanding the Global Spa Industry: Spa Management*. Amsterdam: Butterworth-Heinemann.

Coleman, S., & Eade, J. (Eds.). (2004). *Reframing Pilgrimage: Cultures in Motion*. London/New York: Routledge.

Collins-Kreiner, N. (2010). Researching Pilgrimage: Continuity and Transformations. *Annals of Tourism Research, 37*(2), 440–456.
Coultate, A. (2016, March 18). What's the Way Forward for UK Nightlife? *Resident Advisor*. Retrieved September 10, from https://www.residentadvisor.net/features/2641
Critchlow, A. (2015, May 03). Britain's Sport Industry Hitting Top Form. *The Telegraph*. Retrieved September 17, 2017, from http://www.telegraph.co.uk/finance/11580773/Britains-sport-industry-hitting-top-form.html
Dvorak, D., Saari, S., & Tuominen, T. (Eds.). (2014). *Developing a Competitive Health and Well-being Destination*. Turku: Turku University of Applied Sciences.
Edlin, G., Golanty, E., & McCormack Brown, K. (2000). *Essential for Health and Wellness* (2nd ed.). Sudbury: Jones and Bartlett Publishers.
Ellis, S. (2017). Wellness, Well-Being … and What About Spa? *The Huffington Post*, April 13, 2016, Updated April 09, 2017. Retrieved September 17, 2017, from http://www.huffingtonpost.com/susie-ellis/wellness-wellbeingand-wha_b_9641722.html
Erfurt-Cooper, P., & Cooper, M. (2009). *Health and Wellness Tourism: Spas and Hot Springs*. Bristol: Channel View Publications.
Etzkowitz, H., & Leydesdorff, L. (2000). The Dynamics of Innovation: From National Systems and 'Mode 2' to a Triple Helix of University-Industry-Government Relations. *Research Policy, 29*, 109–123.
European Commission. (2015, February 23). *Growing the European Silver Economy* (Background Paper). Retrieved December 2, 2017, from http://ec.europa.eu/research/innovation-union/pdf/active-healthy-ageing/silvereco.pdf
Florida, R. (2002). *The Rise of the Creative Class: And How It's Transforming Work, Leisure, Community and Everyday Life*. New York: Perseus Book Group.
Gallup, J. W. (1999). *Wellness Centers: A Guide for the Design Professional*. New York: John Wiley & Sons.
Gatchel, R. J., & Schultz, I. Z. (2012). *Handbook of Occupational Health and Wellness*. New York: Springer.
Gaynor, M., & Town, R. J. (2011). Provider Competition. In P. Borras, T. McGuire, & M. Pauly (Eds.), *Handbook of Health Economics* (Vol. 2). Amsterdam: Elsevier.
Gaynor, M., Mostashari, F., & Ginsburg, P. B. (2017). *Making Health Care Markets Work: Competition Policy for Health Care*. Washington, DC: Brookings. Retrieved September 10, 2017, from https://www.brookings.edu/wp-content/uploads/2017/04/gaynor-et-al-final-report-v11.pdf
Glass, R. H., Clifford, N., Harris, B., & Rose, C. (2000, November). *The Role of Public Libraries in Local Economic Development* (Report No. 260). The University of Kansas, Policy Research Institute. Retrieved August 23, 2017, form http://www.ipsr.ku.edu/resrep/pdf/m260.pdf

Global Wellness Institute. (2017, January). *Global Wellness Economy Monitor.* Miami: Global Wellness Institute.
Goldhagen, S. W. (2017). *Welcome to Your World: How the Built Environment Shapes Our Lives* (Kindle Edition). New York: HarperCollins Publishers.
Greene, R. P. (2006). Strong Downtowns and High Amenity Zones as Defining Features of the 21st Century Metropolis: The Case of Chicago. In R. P. Greene, M. J. Bouman, & D. Grammenos (Eds.), *Chicago's Geographies: Metropolis for the 21st Century* (pp. 40–74). Washington, DC: Association of American Geographers.
GSS. (2010, May). *Spas and the Global Wellness Market: Synergies and Opportunities* (SRI International). Miami: Global Spa Summit. Retrieved August 21, 2017, from https://www.sri.com/sites/default/files/publications/gss_sri_spasandwellnessreport_rev_82010.pdf
Ha, I. 'S', & Grunwell, S. (2014). Estimating the Economic Benefits a Business Improvement District Would Provide for a Downtown Central Business District. *Journal of Economics and Economic Education Research, 15*(3), 89–102.
Hamilton-Pennell, C. (2008). Public Libraries and Community Economic Development: Partnering for Success. *Rural Research Report, 18*(10), 1–8. Retrieved August 23, 2017, from http://www.iira.org/wp-content/uploads/2014/08/Public-Libraries-and-Community-Economic-Development-Partnering-for-Success.pdf
Hamilton-Pennell, C. (2009, March 13). Churches and Economic Development. *Supporting Entrepreneurship.* Retrieved August 20, 2017, from https://supportinglocalentrepreneurship.wordpress.com/2009/03/13/churches-and-economic-development/
Harding-Bond, L. (2017). The Intersection of Tech and Wellness. *HuffPost,* January 13, 2016, updated January 13, 2017. Retrieved August 22, 2017, from http://www.huffingtonpost.com/linda-hardingbond/the-intersection-of-tech-_b_8964452.html
Heitner, D. (2015, October 19). Sports Industry to Reach $73.5 Billion by 2019. *Forbes.* Retrieved September 17, 2017, from https://www.forbes.com/sites/darrenheitner/2015/10/19/sports-industry-to-reach-73-5-billion-by-2019/#617ca0f71b4b
Henley, J. (2016, March 21). The Stuff of Night Mayors: Amsterdam Pioneers New Way to Run Cities After Dark. *The Guardian, Cities.* Retrieved September 10, 2017, from https://www.theguardian.com/cities/2016/mar/21/night-mayor-amsterdam-holland-mirik-milan-night-time-commission
Hoad, P. (2015). Welcome to the Naked City: Sun, Swingers and Very Little Shoplifting. *The Guardian, Cities.* Retrieved September 10, 2017, from https://www.theguardian.com/cities/2015/aug/27/naked-city-cap-agde-sun-swingers-shoplifting
Holmes, B., & Douglas, K. (2012). Human Nature: Being Playful. *New Scientist, 214*(2861), 38–40.

Huffman, R. (2015, July 24). Barcelona Bears All. *Barcelona Metropolitan*. Retrieved September 10, 2017, from http://www.barcelona-metropolitan.com/features/barcelona-bares-all/

Jacob, D. (2012). The Eventification of Place: Urban Development and Experience Consumption in Berlin and New York City. *European Urban and Regional Studies, 20*(4), 447–459.

Jacobs, D. (2009, May 1). Promoting Economic Development: Empowering the Church to Empower the Community. *Ministry Matters*. Retrieved August 20, 2017, from http://www.ministrymatters.com/lead/entry/423/promoting-economic-development-empowering-the-church-to-empower-the-community

Kaye, J. (2017). Making Pervasive Computing Technology Pervasive for Health & Wellness in Aging. *Public Policy & Aging Report, 27*(2), 53–61.

Kell, J. (2015, May 22). Lean Times for the Diet Industry. *Fortune*. Retrieved September 10, 2017, from http://fortune.com/2015/05/22/lean-times-for-the-diet-industry/

Kemp, D. (2016, May 4). Brazil's 'Disney World of Sex,' Erotika Land, Sparks Intense Debate. *Inquisitr*. Retrieved September 10, 2017, from https://www.inquisitr.com/3060625/brazils-disney-world-of-sex-erotika-land-sparks-intense-debate/

Kennell, B. (2016). Healthy Food Trends Drive New Products. *HuffPost*, US edition, The Blog, January 10, 2015, Updated September 30, 2016. Retrieved September 10, 2017, from http://www.huffingtonpost.com/brian-kennell/healthy-food-trends-drive_b_8222388.html

Kloosterman, R. C. (2014). Cultural Amenities: Large and Small, Mainstream and Niche—A Conceptual Framework for Cultural Planning in an Age of Austerity. *European Planning Studies, 22*(12), 2510–2525.

Klugman, B. (2007). Locating and Linking Sexuality in Development and Human Rights. *International Journal of Sexual Health, 19*(3), 65–77.

Kotha, R., Kim, P. H., & Alexy, O. (2014, November). Turn Your Science into a Business. *Harvard Business Review* (Issue). Retrieved August 23, 2017, from https://hbr.org/2014/11/turn-your-science-into-a-business

Kotro, T., Timonen, P., Pantzar, M., & Heiskanen, E. (2005). *The Leisure Business and Lifestyle* (Publications 2/2005). Helsinki: National Consumer Research Centre.

Lee Badgett, M. V., Nezhad, S., Waaldijk, K., & Rodgers, Y. V. D. M. (2014, November). *The Relationship Between LGBT Inclusion and Economic Development: An Analysis of Emerging Economies*. The Williams Institute. USAID. Retrieved December 18, 2017, from http://williamsinstitute.law.ucla.edu/wp-content/uploads/lgbt-inclusion-and-development-november-2014.pdf

Lennon, J. J., & Foley, M. (2006). *Dark Tourism: The Attraction of Death and Disaster* (Reprint). London: Thomson.

Lester, R. K. (2005, December 13) *Universities, Innovation, and the Competitiveness of Local Economies: A Summary Report from the Local Innovation Systems Project—Phase I* (Industrial Performance Centre, Local Innovation Systems Project, Working Paper, No. 05-010). Retrieved August 23, 2017, from http://web.mit.edu/lis/papers/LIS05-010.pdf

Louv, R. (2014, February 13). Ten Reasons Why We Need More Contact With Nature. *The Guardian*. Retrieved November 1, 2017, from https://www.theguardian.com/commentisfree/2014/feb/13/10-reasons-why-we-need-more-contact-with-nature

McGinnis, J. M., Williams-Russo, P., & Knickman, J. R. (2002). The Case for More Active Policy Attention to Health Promotion. *Health Affairs, 21*, 278–293.

McMurray, A., & Clendon, J. (2015). *Community Health and Wellness: Primary Health Care in Practice* (5th ed.). Chatswood: Elsevier.

Meltzer, R. (2012). Understanding Business Improvement District Formation: An Analysis of Neighborhoods and Boundaries. *Journal of Urban Economics, 71*(1), 66–78.

Migliaccio, T., & Raskauskas, J. (2016). *Bullying as a Social Experience: Social Factors, Prevention and Intervention*. London/New York: Routledge.

Minford, T. (2016, October 31). The World's Most Famous Cemeteries. *Fodor's Travel*. Retrieved August 21, 2017, from http://www.fodors.com/news/arts-culture/smithsonian-exhibit-showcases-sylvia-plaths-original-artwork

Miron, M. (2017, January). Phoenix's North Seventh Street: Healthy, Green Living Options Galore. *Natural Awakenings* (Phoenix Edition). Retrieved August 23, 2017, from http://www.naturalaz.com/ARIZ/January-2017/Phoenixs-North-Seventh-Street-Healthy-Green-Living-Options-Galore/

Monteiro, S., & Carayannis, E. G. (Eds.). (2017). *The Quadruple Innovation Helix Nexus: A Smart Growth Model, Quantitative Empirical Validation and Operationalization for OECD Countries*. New York: Palgrave Macmillan.

Moos, R. H. (2003). Social Contexts: Transcending Their Power and Their Fragility. *American Journal of Community Psychology, 31*(1–2), 1–13.

Morgentaler, A. (2013). *Why Men Fake It: The Totally Unexpected Truth About Men and Sex*. New York: Henry Holt and Company.

Munson, S. A., Lauterbach, D., Newman, M. W., & Resnick, P. (2010). Happier Together: Integrating a Wellness Application into a Social Network Site. In T. Ploug, P. Hasle, H. Oinas-Kukkonen (Eds.), *Persuasive Technology*, Lecture Notes in Computer Science (Vol. 6137, pp. 27–39). Berlin: Springer.

Murano, G. (2016, June 6). 8 Amazing Adult Only Parks & Attractions. *Oddee*. Retrieved September 10, 2017, from http://www.oddee.com/item_99718.aspx

Near Southside, Inc. (n/a). *Medical District* (Website). Retrieved September 15, 2017, from https://www.nearsouthsidefw.org/medical-district.html

Nestpick.com. (n/a). *Best LGBT Cities 2017* (Website). Retrieved October 24, 2017, from https://www.nestpick.com/best-lgbt-cities/

Nielsen. (2014, June 10). iHealth: How Consumers Are Using Tech to Stay Healthy. *Nielsen, Media*. The Nielsen Company (US), LLC. Retrieved August 22, 2017, from http://www.nielsen.com/us/en/insights/news/2014/ihealth-how-consumers-are-using-tech-to-stay-healthy.html

Oldenburg, R. (1989). *The Great Good Place: Cafes, Coffee Shops, Community Centers, Beauty Parlors, General Stores, Bars, Hangouts, and How They Get You Through the Day*. New York: Paragon House.

Orcutt, A. (2012, January 4). World's Most-Visited Sacred Sites. *Travel + Leisure*. Retrieved August 21, 2017, from http://www.travelandleisure.com/slideshows/worlds-most-visited-sacred-sites

Orji, R., & Moffatt, K. (2016). Persuasive Technology for Health and Wellness: State-of-the-Art and Emerging Trends. *Health Informatics Journal* (First Published May 31, 2016). https://doi.org/10.1177/1460458216650979

Oxford Dictionaries. (2017). *Dictionary* (Website). Oxford: Oxford University Press. Retrieved August 18, 2017, from https://en.oxforddictionaries.com/

Ozanian, M. (2017, June 6). The World's Most Valuable Soccer Teams 2017. *Forbes*. Retrieved September 17, 2017, from https://www.forbes.com/sites/mikeozanian/2017/06/06/the-worlds-most-valuable-soccer-teams-2017/#16652c5977ea

Packham J., Price S., & Harris, T. R. (2006). *The Impact of the Local Health Care System on the Humboldt County Economy* (Technical Report UCED 2005/06-38). Reno: University of Nevada, University Center for Economic Development. Retrieved August 20, 2017, from https://www.unr.edu/Documents/business/uced/technical-reports/humboldt/health-sector-impacts-humboldt.pdf

PBS. (2017, March 21). Inclusive Wellness Center Is an Oasis for a Neighborhood Left Behind. *PBS NewsHour*. Retrieved September 10, 2017, from http://www.pbs.org/newshour/bb/inclusive-wellness-center-oasis-neighborhood-left-behind/

Pillay, P. (2011). *Higher Education and Economic Development. Literature Review* (PDF File).Wynberg: Centre for Higher Education Transformation (CHET). Retrieved August 23, 2017, from https://chet.org.za/files/uploads/reports/Pillay%202010%20HE%20and%20Economic%20Development%20Literature%20Review.pdf

Polanyi, M. (1967). *The Tacit Dimension*. New York: Anchor Books.

Raphael, R. (2017, June 30). Namaste En Masse: Can Wellness Festivals Grow as Big as Coachella? *Fast Company*. Retrieved September 1, 2017, from https://www.fastcompany.com/40421458/namaste-en-masse-can-wellness-festivals-grow-as-big-as-coachella

Reed, G. J. (1994). *Economic Empowerment through the Church: A Blueprint for Progressive Community Development*. Grand Rapids: Zondervan Publishing House.

Reese, R. F., & Myers, J. E. (2012). EcoWellness: The Missing Factor in Holistic Wellness Models. *Journal of Counseling and Development, 90*(4), 400–407.

Research and Markets. (2015, February). *Weight Loss and Weight Management Market by Equipment, Surgical Equipment, Diet, Weight Loss Services—Forecast to 2019*. Retrieved September 10, 2017, from https://www.researchandmarkets.com/research/xvpflx/weight_loss_and

Rose, J. F. P. (2016). *The Well-Tempered City: What Modern Science, Ancient Civilizations, and Human Nature Teach Us About the Future of Urban Life*. New York: Harper Wave.

Rudolph, L., Caplan, J., Ben-Moshe, K., & Dillon, L. (2013). *Health in All Policies: A Guide for State and Local Governments*. Washington, DC/Oakland: American Public Health Association/Public Health Institute. Retrieved August 28, 2017, from https://www.phi.org/uploads/files/Health_in_All_Policies-A_Guide_for_State_and_Local_Governments.pdf

Schuch, S. (2015, January 18). Flint Health Organizations Bring 'Wellness Hub' to Flint Farmers' Market to Educate Community. *MLive*. Retrieved September 10, 2017, from http://www.mlive.com/news/flint/index.ssf/2015/01/flint_health_organizations_bri.html

Schueller, S. M. (2009). Promoting Wellness: Integrating Community and Positive Psychology. *Journal of Community Psychology, 37*(7), 922–937.

Scipioni, J. (2016, May 5). Fertile Farmlands in the Heart of NYC and Chicago? *Fox Business*. Retrieved November 28, 2017, from http://www.foxbusiness.com/features/2016/05/05/fertile-farmlands-in-heart-nyc-and-chicago.html

Scruggs, G. (2017, May 1). Lessons from Amsterdam's 'Night Mayor'. *Citiscope*. Retrieved September 10, 2017, from http://citiscope.org/story/2017/lessons-amsterdams-night-mayor

Sena, M. (n/a). Fitness Industry Analysis 2017—Cost & Trends. *FranchiseHelp*. Retrieved September 10, 2017, from https://www.franchisehelp.com/industry-reports/fitness-industry-report/

Skelton, P. (2017, September 13). Amsterdam Drug Policy. *Amsterdam.info*. Retrieved September 10, 2017, from https://www.amsterdam.info/drugs/

Smith, M., & Puczkó, L. (2009). *Health and Wellness Tourism* (2nd ed.). Oxford: Butterworth-Heinemann.

Starr, A. (2015, January 19). 15 of the World's Most Expensive and Luxurious Brothels. *The Richest*. Retrieved November 27, 2017, from https://www.therichest.com/luxury/most-expensive/15-of-the-worlds-most-expensive-and-luxurious-brothels/

Taylor, M. (2011). *Public Policy in the Community* (2nd ed.). Basingstoke: Palgrave Macmillan.

Teshler, Y. (2016, June 9). Wellness Wasteland: Technology Isn't Where We Need It Most. *Forbes*. Retrieved August 22, 2017, from https://www.forbes.com/sites/moorinsights/2016/06/09/wellness-wasteland-technology-isnt-where-we-need-it-most/#2094d0554f37

The Telegraph. (2012, April 20). Want to Cheer Yourself Up? Go for a Walk in a Cemetery. Retrieved August 21, 2017, from http://www.telegraph.co.uk/news/newstopics/howaboutthat/9216244/Want-to-cheer-yourself-up-go-for-a-walk-in-a-cemetery.html

Thrall, G. I. (2002). *Business Geography and New Real Estate Market Analysis*. Oxford: Oxford University Press.

Torrance, C. (2011, Spring). The Post Genomic Era; What Does It All Mean? *Drug Discovery World (DDW), Personalised Medicine*. Retrieved September 9, 2017, from http://www.ddw-online.com/personalised-medicine/p142740-the-post-genomic-era%3B-what-does-it-all-mean-spring-11.html

Troutman, A., & Benjamin, G. C. (2013). Preface. In L. Rudolph, J. Caplan, K. Ben-Moshe, & L. Dillon (Eds.), *Health in All Policies: A Guide for State and Local Governments* (p. 1). Washington, DC/Oakland: American Public Health Association/Public Health Institute. Retrieved August 28, 2017, from https://www.phi.org/uploads/files/Health_in_All_Policies-A_Guide_for_State_and_Local_Governments.pdf

Tynan, D. (2008, October 31). Shopping IS Good for You: How Manolos Can Save Your Life. *Women's Health*. Retrieved December 27, 2017, from https://www.womenshealthmag.com/life/shopping-and-happiness

Valdez, J. (2016, January 4). Our Top 10 Apps for Health & Wellness. *Rewire Me*. Retrieved August 22, 2017, from https://www.rewireme.com/wellness/top-10-apps-health-wellness/

Vilhelmsson, A. (2017). Value-Based Health Care Delivery, Preventive Medicine and the Medicalization of Public Health. *Cureus, 9*(3), e1063. https://doi.org/10.7759/cureus.1063

Vita Health and Wellness District. (2013, August). Vita: Care. Grow. Aspire. Health & Wellness District in Stamford, CT. City of Stamford. Charter Oak Communities. Stamford Hospital. Retrieved August 23, 2017, http://vitastamford.com/wp-content/themes/vita/media/VITA_2013_REPORT.pdf

Vogt, H., Hofmann, B., & Getz, L. (2016). The New Holism: P4 Systems Medicine and the Medicalization of Health and Life Itself. *Medicine, Health Care, and Philosophy, 19*(2), 307–323.

Ward, H., & Aral, S. O. (2006). Globalisation, the Sex Industry, and Health. *Sexually Transmitted Infections, 82*(5), 345–347.

WGSN Insider. (2017, May 12). Health, Fitness and Wellness: Heritage Retailers Want You to Work Out in Store. *WGSN Insider*. Retrieved August 21, 2017, from https://www.wgsn.com/blogs/health-fitness-and-wellness-heritage-retail-wants-you-to-work-out-in-store/

Wharton, C., Fenwick, J., & Fawcett, H. (2010). Public Policy in the Party City: The Spectacle of Culture, Gender, and Locality. *International Journal of Public Administration, 33*(14), 779–789.

Williams, A. (1987). Health Economics: The Cheerful Face of the Dismal Science? In A. Williams (Ed.), *Health and Economics. Proceedings of Section F (Economics) of the British Association for the Advancement of Science, Bristol, 1986* (pp. 1–11). London: Palgrave Macmillan.

Wilson, J. (2014, October 7). 'Suicide Tourism' to Switzerland Has Doubled Since 2009. *CNN*. Retrieved October 25, 2017, from http://edition.cnn.com/2014/08/20/health/suicide-tourism-switzerland/index.html

Wolf, K. L. (2004). Public Value of Nature: Economics of Urban Trees, Parks and Open Space. In D. Miller, & J. A. Wise (Eds.), *Design with Spirit. Proceedings of the 35th Annual Conference of the Environmental Design Research Association*. Edmond: Environmental Design Research Association. Retrieved August 22, 2017, from https://www.naturewithin.info/Policy/EDRA_Value.pdf

Young, M. M. (2010). Twitter Me: Using Micro-Blogging to Motivate Teenagers to Exercise. In R. Winter, Z. J. Leon, & S. Aier (Eds.), *Global Perspectives on Design Science Research*, Lecture Notes in Computer Science (Vol. 6105, pp. 439–448). Berlin: Springer.

CHAPTER 6

Wellness City Strategies in Local–Global Dialectic

Abstract This chapter takes a close view of wellness city strategies in the context of global competition between cities by focusing on three types of strategy: smart, community-driven wellness city strategies; tourist attraction-oriented wellness city strategies; and innovative, export-driven wellness city strategies. Each is briefly introduced and then exemplified by a few real-life case descriptions, including: smart wellness cities in Japan; Health Village in Tampere, Finland; Water Street Tampa, Florida; Mines Wellness City in Malaysia; Dubai Healthcare City in Dubai, UAE; Jeju Healthcare Town in Jeju Island, South Korea; a welfare cluster in Sendai, Japan; a health and high-tech integration in Austin, Texas; and a health care business incubator in Lisbon, Portugal.

Keywords Strategy • Smart city • Health care • Tourism • Export • Smart wellness city

This chapter concretizes the discussion about wellness-oriented economic development by presenting cases of the making of real-life wellness cities. The cases are grouped on the basis of three ideal types of strategy for coping with the local–global dialectic: (1) community-based developments that rely on local assets, urban infrastructures, and innovative real estate business built essentially on the needs of old and new residents; (2) consumption-driven developments that aim to attract tourists to a locality;

A.-V. Anttiroiko, *Wellness City*,
https://doi.org/10.1007/978-3-319-75562-5_6

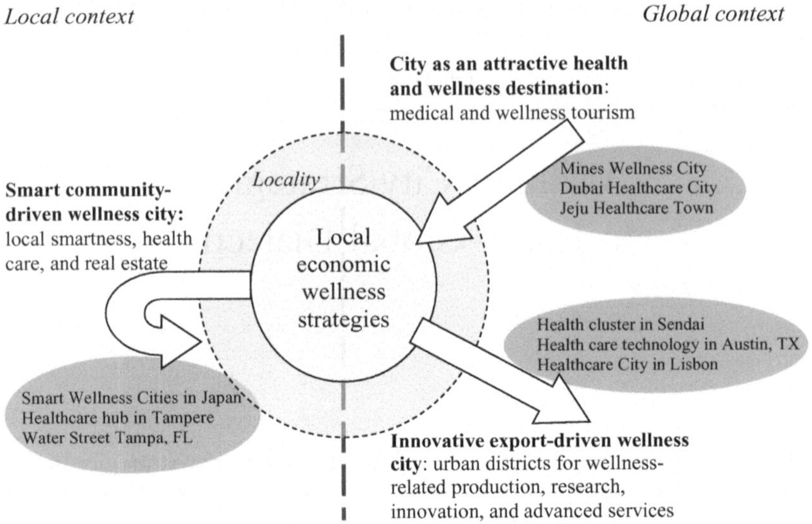

Fig. 6.1 Wellness and three aspects of local–global dialectic. (Source: Applied from Anttiroiko 2015)

and (3) innovative export-driven developments that focus on scientific research, high technology, and advanced services, and that seek profits by meeting the demand for high-value knowledge, products, and business-to-business services in the global wellness market (see Fig. 6.1).

Smart Community-Driven Wellness City Developments

Community-driven wellness city strategies put community health first, or at least their profit-making strategies are based on urban infrastructures, real estate, and amenities designed to attract and serve wellness-oriented inhabitants. The idea is to work at the grassroots level to create pleasant environments that are conducive to health, while at the same time enhancing real estate businesses and creating conditions for endogenous economic growth. Healthier people means a healthier workforce and less pressure on "illness care" in the health care system. This implies synergies between conventional community health and emerging holistic urban wellness, which have a special value in local economic development.

A community-oriented approach is an underlying element in urban regeneration and revitalization projects, encompassing business improvement districts and similar developments. Such developments have direct connections to the wellness-oriented real estate sector, which is an essential aspect of community-driven wellness city development. Such business is rooted in locality while at the same time being highly dependent on consumption trends, growth prospects, and changes in competitive local–global settings. Such a business-oriented community development can be based on various local assets, of which we will discuss the three most prominent: (1) health-oriented local development with health care and wellness governance, integration, and promotion as its primary mission; (2) technology-driven development associated with smart health and wellness; and (3) real estate and community-building efforts, in which real estate business seeks ways to utilize the demand for a healthy environment and a wellness-oriented lifestyle.

Wellness Through Service Integration

Due to the expansion of the health care sector in the post-war years and the more recent growth in wellness industries, there is a historically unique opportunity to create a synergistic relationship between these two paradigms with significant implications for local economic development. Major hospitals and health care centers have evolved through the decades into important local institutions. Their primary task is to provide special care for patients in their neighborhood or wider catchment areas, but their actual role goes beyond that. They are in many cases local anchor institutions serving as centers of expertise, integrators of institutional resources, and employers that hire local workers (Jablow 2017).

Health care institutions should escape their silo mentality and better integrate with institutions and communities around them, which is conducive to affecting the determinants of health and indirectly enhancing local development opportunities. Such a need is most prominent in *public health*, in which the need for building collaboration with the wider medical and health care delivery system has long been emphasized (Van Gorder 2015). The same goes for the whole health care system, which should allow greater organizational flexibility and adaptation to local context (Suter et al. 2009). In all, the productive alignment of medical services with *public health* has been long desired but infrequently experienced. Pursuing this goal would bring the medical paradigm closer to the wellness paradigm and at the same time mark a move towards a better understanding of the value of co-creation in the given context (Beaglehole et al. 2004).

The need to integrate a siloed health care sector has been addressed in various ways in health care reforms. In the USA, for example, there has long been a need to reform the health care system and, as a part of that agenda, to encourage the building of collaborative models of care delivery (Burton and Haughom n/a). Healthcare Innovation Zones centered around Academic Medical Centers, Accountable Care Organizations, medical homes, and other innovative approaches to care are important but are not enough for a radical transformation (Ellis and Razavi 2012). A reform agenda that is confined to existing health care systems and a medical paradigm is more about cutting costs and streamlining supply-side activities than *reinventing health care*. In the developed country context, the latter requires that we pay more attention to the causes and consequences of chronic diseases, which simply cannot be solved within a conventional medical paradigm (Kresser 2017). Rather, we need *service integration* within a *comprehensive wellness policy*, which requires that: (1) contextual, community, and lifestyle dimensions are proactively taken into account in health care, which implies a transition from cure-based to prevention-based systems; (2) health and wellness centers and wellness coaching are included in the comprehensive local wellness policy agenda; (3) beside conventional Western medicine complementary, alternative, and traditional medicine and a range of wellness services are utilized when appropriate from the point of view of personalized, preventive, or rehabilitative health care (e.g. Lim et al. 2013); and (4) the service delivery system will be redesigned to become community-oriented, co-creative, and collaborative (cf. Kresser 2017; Porter and Lee 2013). Such a transformation implies a move away from a fragmented, supply-driven health care system, organized around what physicians do, towards a patient-centered service ecosystem based on holistic view of patients' conditions and needs, which would contribute to a parallel shift from the volume of services to the patient outcomes (Porter and Lee 2013).

Even if integration is a standard solution to problems of fragmentation, it is actually a rather complicated matter in health care (Anttiroiko and Valkama 2016). Its rationale is to create value by changing the behavior of patients and healthcare providers in ways that improve clinical outcomes, reduce costs, and provide a better experience for all. There are many drivers behind such developments. From our point of view the most interesting one is greater *consumer engagement*, which urges a seamless care experience and increases the legitimacy of the patient/caregiver relation in treatment choices and ongoing care. The emphasis can be either on *episodes of care* or on *continuous care*, which approach the integration issue from different ends of the "medical continuum" (Retterath et al. 2013). However, such a bipolar model could be extended in two directions. First, it could be supported by holistic *wellness care* in various dedicated environments. Second, it could be connected with *community care*, which includes community health, preventive care, the promotion of holistic health, active participation of community members, and support for local inhabitants to meet their needs from welfare services (cf. White and Harris 2001). This four-layer integration model is presented in Fig. 6.2.

Building Smart Wellness Cities

The Wellness++, or high value-added wellness sector is largely based on hospitals with a range of medical services and medically and professionally oriented wellness centers, on the one hand, and research-intensive industries relating to health care equipment, pharmaceuticals, biotechnology, and life sciences, on the other. Their connection with urban development can be viewed through various frameworks, of which arguably the most

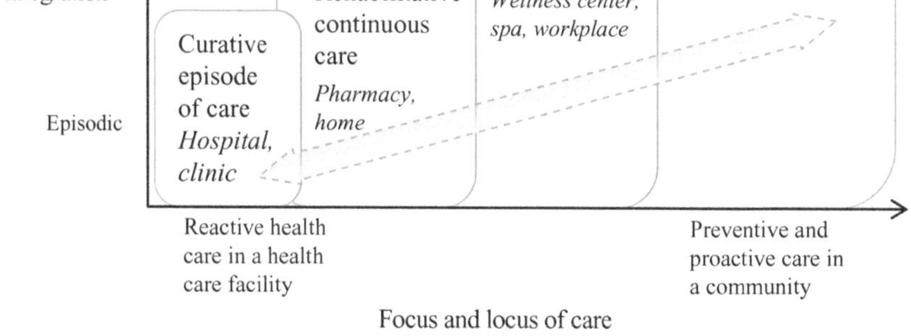

Fig. 6.2 Value creation and integration within health continuum

interesting one is the *smart city* (Komninos 2015; Murgante and Borruso 2015; Anttiroiko et al. 2013; Angelidou 2015). It highlights the importance of technological developments in building smartness into urban systems and environments that are conducive to urban wellness.

Smart city refers to a multi-dimensional urban development model, in which technological advancements are used to enhance collective intelligence and systemic capabilities to increase competitiveness, effectiveness, quality of life, and sustainability in an urban community (Anttiroiko 2016). A necessary condition for smart city development is a collaborative setting, which is of vital importance for the development of urban wellness. This is one of the most interesting aspects of a smart city framework with regard to wellness as it explicitly points to the relevance of a systemic and contextual approach that conditions the value co-creation within a complex health and wellness service ecosystem with cyber-physical systems and related platforms as its facilitative nodes (Komninos 2016; Glushko 2010; Mikusz 2015). An emerging health service ecosystem utilizes a range of new technologies, such as ambient assisted living, to exploit ICTs in personal health care and telehealth systems, internet-of-things (IoT) platforms used for remote monitoring and medical device integration, pervasive and ubiquitous technologies to enable remote control of wellness applications and systems, and Big Data to be used to predict epidemics, cure disease, and improve quality of life (e.g. Memon et al. 2014).

Previously mentioned applications, platforms, and systems pave the way for a deeper transformation in urban health and wellness. The first step is the creation of smart platforms, such as SMART Health IT, which is an open standards-based technology platform that enables innovators to create applications that seamlessly and securely run across the health care system (on SMART application platforms for health care, see https://smarthealthit.org/). Emerging IoT solutions in health care manifest the same trend, for with its sensing, analytics, and visualization tools they redefine how the elements of socio-technical systems in health care interact to deliver health care solutions (Bhatt et al. 2017). In the same vain, Big Data technologies will improve the capability of health care machinery to utilize the large pool of genomic, clinical, behavioral, and other relevant health care data for better service (Raghupathi and Raghupathi 2014; Wang and Alexander 2015). Smart technologies may even take us beyond the data analytics capability, remote control of infrastructures, and smartening up of interaction by building "conscious cities." In the future, urban infrastructures and systems may alleviate stress, anxiety, and boredom; be aware of the personalities and even moods of local inhabitants and respond to them accordingly; and help to increase the feeling of care and inclusiveness (Palti and Bar 2015). We are, however, only at the beginning of a long journey towards truly smart wellness cities.

Building Wellness Communities

Even if community-building is essentially a social process, our interest here is in the building of physical environments that support urban wellness. To be more precise, our focus is on real estate business, which is a key stakeholder in locality development. One of the areas of tension that has special relevance for our discussion is that while local development used to be determined locally and markets were dominated by local real estate developers, today both greenfield developments and the improvement of existing urban areas—the revitalization of distressed urban areas, improvements in neighborhoods and business districts, and the renewal of areas that are going through gentrification—attract global speculative investors and developers, which changes the role of the real estate sector as regards both locally based property owners and developers and local governments (cf. Healey 1994). However, even if some part of the economy seems to be hyper-speculative and occasionally disengaged from the real value creation processes, lifestyle real estate and wellness-oriented community property development seems to be locally engaged and socially responsive, most likely due to the fact that to look credible, wellness-oriented real estate businesses must apply corporate values and culture that resonate to a degree with a holistic view of health, community orientation, and sustainability.

The Global Wellness Institute (GWI) has highlighted the role of wellness real estate and communities as a part of a wellness cluster. It defines wellness lifestyle real estate as "homes and communities expressly designed for residents' physical, mental, social and environmental health" (Global Wellness Institute 2017). *Wellness communities*, in turn, are communities that are developed proactively with the holistic health of its residents, health-promoting environment, and a sense of community in mind. Such communities may take various forms and operate at different scales, including buildings, quarters, neighborhoods, city districts, and even entire cities. It is difficult to estimate the size of this part of the wellness economy, but GWI assumes that the global market for wellness communities and lifestyle real estate was some USD 119 billion in 2015, concentrated primarily in North America, Europe, and Asia-Pacific.

Wellness communities are extremely diverse, depending on the founder's or developer's vision, economic conditions, and community characteristics. Examples are: Serenbe in a semi-rural area outside Atlanta, Georgia, which reflects the ideas of new urbanism and emphasizes connections to agriculture; Lake Nona, a mixed-use planned community in Orlando, Florida developed by Lake Nona Property Holdings, including among others Lake Nona Golf & Country Club, a life sciences cluster known as Lake Nona Medical City, and an array of retail centers, recreational facilities, and residential options; and BedZED or Beddington Zero Energy Development in Hackbridge, London Borough of Sutton, England, which is an environmentally friendly housing development that aims to become a zero-carbon city (Global Wellness Institute 2016a).

The minimum criteria for a *wellness community* include: (1) environmental consciousness; (2) commitment to holistic health and wellness as shown by providing residents with opportunities to proactively take care of themselves and enhance their overall well-being and quality of life; and (3) enhancing social connections by physical and programmatic elements that foster intergenerational socialization and the sense of community (Global Wellness Institute 2016b). A GWI roundtable on the wellness lifestyle real estate sector identified the following points concerning the principles to guide the future development of the wellness real estate business (Global Wellness Institute 2016a; 2017):

1) Gather and communicate metrics—also take a total "return-on-wellness" into account
2) Focus on holistic wellness living, not just gyms and spas
3) Expand the concept to lower-income communities
4) Focus less narrowly on greenfield developments
5) Foster human connection as a response to the global age of loneliness
6) Embrace multi-generational living
7) Ensure walkability and easy access to work, schools, and urban amenities
8) Simplicity = Real Wellness
9) Science will transform future approaches
10) Healthy growth ahead (i.e. prospects for wellness real estate business are promising).

Sources of demand for lifestyle properties and wellness communities may arise from people who desire a healthy life, who are looking for a retirement place by the sea, who seek a new home near a golf course or other hobby, or who seek authenticity or aesthetics from a historic city. Many such people look for new homes or communities with health and well-being in mind, which means that they pay attention to healthy and safe environments, health-promoting amenities, proximity to health and wellness institutions, and possibly even a wellness-minded community, which reflects values and aspirations derived from a holistic view of health. Another inherent feature of wellness communities is an urban design that aims at sustainability and creating compact, diverse, and walkable urban environments (EPA 2012).

Wellness Through Lifestyle Changes: Smart Wellness Cities in Japan

Special platforms for local development in Japan are Comprehensive Special Zones, which the government set up to provide focused support through national and regional policy resources to pioneering initiatives with high potential for providing groundbreaking social and economic benefits. Such zones include: Okayama New Health Care Style Special Zone in Okayama city; Medical Valley stretching from Oita to Miyazaki in Eastern Kyushu; and a medical and welfare zone in Kagawa. The last one is a comprehensive medical welfare zone initiated in the early 2010s. Beside enhancing healthy lives for residents, especially in the islands of the prefecture, by smartening up the performance, collaboration, and effectiveness of local health institutions through remote medical care systems, it serves at the same time as a wellness-oriented growth strategy (V-cube n/a).

Japan has paid special attention to the building of technology-facilitated platforms and environments that go beyond stand-alone solutions and individual applications. That is where the idea of smart city comes into the picture. It is about wellness embedded in techno-savvy urban environments in a persuasive, ubiquitous, and interconnected way. We have seen only weak signals of such a development so far, but the building of embedded and interconnected smart environments is slowly emerging, connecting wellness with such technology trends as the IoT, ubiquitous technologies, augmented reality, and Big Data (see Komninos 2015).

An example of this trend is the utilization of the IoT in supporting community health. For instance, the Aizuwakamatsu Smart Wellness City IoT Healthcare Platform Project aimed to develop a safe, open commons healthcare IoT platform in the city of Aizuwakamatsu for local governments, hospitals, and companies, with the idea of linking devices, data, and services for better health informatics and streamlined service processes. Another example is the project for charging IoT health services with incentives piloted in the cities of Mitsuke, Date, Takaishi, Ohtawara, Urayasu, and Okayama in different parts of Japan. It aimed to develop an IoT health service model to be integrated with health check-up data possessed by those covered by national insurance, or participants with personal data obtained via an active mass meter, a body composition monitor, or other device, to evaluate fitness efforts and their results (see Fig. 6.3). The project examined the willingness of people to continue to use the service when it switches from free to fee-charging. It also assessed the effect of these IoT-enabled practices on medical expenditure (midika-iot.jp n/a).

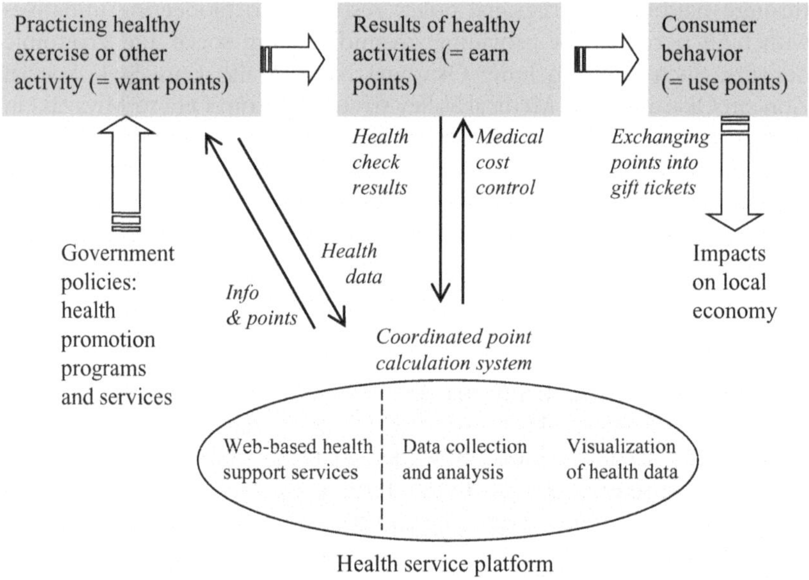

Fig. 6.3 Personal health service platform and IoT health service design. (Source: Modified from midika-iot.jp n/a)

Another much-discussed case is the Fujisawa Sustainable Smart Town—aka Fujisawa SST—a state-of-the-art smart town located in the former Panasonic plant site in Fujisawa city, Kanagawa prefecture (see http://fujisawasst.com/EN/project/). It is a partnership-based project within which partner companies promote advanced initiatives piloted in the city district with some 1000 households. Its underlying idea is that the city and its design should reflect the actual lifestyles of its citizens. The initial visionary plan and guidelines were supplemented by residents' objectives and feedback, and sharing their views of how to achieve a higher quality of life. The town management company is supposed to take residents' views into consideration, incorporate selected new features and technologies into the service palette of the district, and continuously support the sustainable evolution of the town. Such innovative lifestyle-based systems are expected to revitalize people's lives in the community in terms of wellness and other relevant aspects of daily life. One area of the Fujisawa SST is called Wellness Square, which is a concentration of elderly care facilities, clinics, nurseries, day care centers, and preparatory schools (Tokoro 2016, 61).

Beside artificial intelligence and digital platforms, there emerged a movement in Japan in the 2010s, which was less about technology and more about social intelligence and lifestyle. It emerged through several wellness zones and projects, which arose from the pressing needs of an aging society to shift from conventional health care to holistic wellness. Japan is developing into a sustainable society with a focus on illness prevention and health promotion, that seems necessary due to the rapidly rising average age, the share of senior citizens in the nation's population, and their profound impact on national and local economies. The most widely used label for such a movement is *Smart Wellness City*, which points to an urban setting where residents are encouraged to promote their health by changing their lifestyles, for example, walking as part of their daily routine. Local governments, together with industry and academia, have also established designated zones that aim to facilitate behavioral changes among residents (Kume 2017).

An illuminating example of such activities was the Six-City-Partnership Smart Wellness Point Project that lasted from December 2014 to March 2017. It was an experimental project that aimed to attract both willing and reluctant citizens to join healthy walking practices. Tsukuba Wellness Research Inc., a company that analyzes health measures and policies based on medical science data, took the lead in the project and facilitated the involvement of the partner cities of Date, Ohtawara, Mitsuke, Urayasu,

Takaishi, and Okayama. Did the points project make a difference? According to surveys of the Japanese National Health Insurance program conducted before and after the launch of the project, the total annual medical costs of the six participating cities were reduced by 43,000 yen (about USD 384) per person in their 60s, and 97,000 yen (about USD 866) per person in their 70s or older. The estimated spillover effects on the local economy amounted to 120 million yen (about USD 1.07 million). The net profit for the entire project was thus estimated to be in the region of 470 million yen (about USD 4.2 million) (Kume 2017). Such results indicate the potential for the application of health and wellness technologies, emerging health and wellness systems, and related lifestyle changes, which will be fully realized if and when cities are able to create seamless and connected service innovation and co-creation ecosystems.

Health Care Hub in a Smart City: Tampere, Finland

Western medicine and medical equipment reflect a scientific approach to health (Bhargava and Bhargava 2007). This has created a unique feature in urban social and institutional infrastructures throughout the developed world. Major hospitals and health care centers have become important local institutions as concentrations of expertise and resources, and at the same time as large segments of the economy (Jablow 2017). When such health and wellness concentrations grow, they offer inherent business opportunities—even though within regulated and institutionalized environments operating primarily as professionally organized hierarchies. An interesting case, where a local health care system evolved from a local service complex into a smart health care hub, is the city of Tampere, Finland.

Tampere is a middle-sized city with an industrial heritage, as indicated by its nickname, Manse, derived from Manchester of Finland. It became a city of several large industrial sites in the nineteenth century, and evolved into one of the largest cities of the Finnish welfare society, boosted by public sector expansion after World War II. Its two universities, technology park, and university hospital created a natural institutional basis for clustering around medical expertise, health care technologies, and life sciences. Its manufacturing-oriented industrial policy evolved towards high technology in the 1980s. During the following decade the guiding idea was the promotion of a digital economy and governance, and in the latter half of the 2000s the development of biotechnology and creative industries were the most prominent novel elements in the city's economic development policy (Kasvio and Anttiroiko 2005). Smart city became a new framework for the city's development activities in the latter half of the 2010s.

Smart Tampere is a local economic vitality program for 2017–2021 that promotes digitalization and sustainable development. It has two major pillars: the ecosystem program comprising the development of seven themes; while the digitalization program focuses on the digitalization of local public services. Its aim is to make Tampere an internationally known smart city, which attracts firms and talent, and creates new business opportunities within its smart business, service, and innovation ecosystems (see http://smarttampere.fi/).

One of the themes of the ecosystem program is *smart health*. Its focus is to identify and prepare new operational models and pilots in collaboration between companies, city government, and the regional hospital district. The approach of the program is built on co-creation, flexible solutions, and agile experimentation to be applied to the development and provision of social and health care services. The digitalization program supports such activities by promoting the adoption of ICT in local public services. The vision is that by 2025 all residents of the city will use primarily digital services, including social and health services. The city is dedicated to promoting transparency and integrating digital solutions, and set up pilots that focus on self-care and health-promoting activities. This creates natural connections with wellness trends and highlights the importance of the digitalization of health and well-being data and its utilization. New digital services are designed to support three areas of health in particular, which all resonate with wellness discourse:

- exercise and preventive services
- self-directed care, self-service, and health care at home
- future hospitals and well-being centers.

The smart health development in Tampere has a particular geographical hotspot, Health Village, which consists of Kauppi university hospital campus, science and business park, and surrounding Kauppi outdoors sports and recreation area. It developed quickly in the 2000s from an idea into a half a billion euro investment project. Its clinical core is Tampere University Hospital supported by a range of clinical services. The "collaborative circle" surrounding this core comprises a science and business park, a patient hotel, and other services and knowledge institutions. The key facilitator in this development is FinnMedi Oy, a local intermediary company. Due to the institutionally thick environment, FinnMedi has a large pool of social, scientific, technological, biomedical, and medical expertise, which together with close connections with business has made it a rapidly growing life science center. FinnMedi's mission is to bring companies closer to clinics by providing services relating to research commercialization, business development, clinical research, infrastructure development, and support for research, innovators, and startups (Salomaa 2015).

Tampere Health Village is meant to become a health and wellness village of the future, which brings health technologies, health care, and wellness to the same area. Its initial funding has been provided by local and regional governments, the regional hospital district, and local higher education institutions. Concerning business promotion, a new Health HUB has been opened in the Kauppi campus as a part of the Tampere Health Village program. The HUB is a meeting place for health care firms, clinicians, researchers, developers, and service users. Working together is an unofficial motto of this venture, as it provides resources for developing ideas into innovations and profitable businesses. It offers both physical sites and online working rooms, which allows collaboration irrespective of people's actual locations.

Towards a Smart Wellness City District: Water Street Tampa

A true paradigm shift in urban wellness requires that we look beyond both destination development and urban engineering, that is, that we aspire to, envision, and dream about new forms of urban life. Our pressing problems and challenges relating to urban living co-exist with unprecedented opportunities backed up by wealth and technological advancements, which calls for new ideas about cities, usually combining such elements as smartness, sustainability, social inclusion, livability, and connectedness (Komninos 2015; Kenneally et al. 2014; Polizer 2017). This visionary view of cities incorporates various elements into the big picture, reminding us of the potential of the use of smart technologies and systems in promoting holistic health at personal, family, neighborhood, and city levels.

An example of this is Water Street Tampa (WST), the ten-year, USD 3 billion, mixed-use, inner city development project by Strategic Property Partners, LLC—the real estate firm backed up by billionaire Jeffrey N. Vinik and Bill Gates' asset management company Cascade Investment—in downtown

Tampa, Florida. It has a focus on bringing housing, retail, entertainment, and office space together for a novel experience in urban living (see https://waterstreettampa.com/). WST became news because of its fresh lifestyle and wellness-oriented approach to downtown development. The real estate business core of the project, which utilizes the amenities of the downtown riverside area, is laced with livability, health, and wellness. It is said that for the first time it is not just an intelligent building or safe environment in the making, but the world's first "wellness district" designed to make its residents healthier (Griffin 2017).

The wellness district standards are to be incorporated into Strategic Property Partners' 50-acre redevelopment area, anchored around the Amalie Arena, which is home to Jeff Vinik's Tampa Bay Lightning hockey team and the Tampa Bay Storm football team. The design of wellness aims to make the neighborhood walkable, have abundant green space, and provide access to healthy food and to the amenities of the waterfront area to enhance the quality of life (March 2016). Phase one of the project will be completed by the early 2020s, including: some 1000 residential units; a new luxury hotel; retail, restaurant, and entertainment venues; the University of South Florida Morsani College of Medicine and Heart Institute; and an adjoining office tower for health-related businesses (March 2016; Grauerholz 2016).

The WST is designed to become the world's first WELL-Certified city district. It means that it is the first district-wide application of the WELL Building Standard, which in turn is the world's first building standard focused exclusively on human health and wellness. It was developed to fulfill a 2012 Clinton Global Initiative (CGI) Commitment to Action to improve the way people live indoors, and this new commitment builds on WELL and tackles the even greater challenge of creating city-scale developments built for health and wellness. The project, informed by the WELL Building Standard, will reflect seven categories that relate to health in the built environment: air, water, nourishment, light, fitness, comfort, and mind. The overall aim is to create a community that promotes nutrition, fitness, mood, sleep patterns, and performance for residents and visitors (Grauerholz 2016). There is some empirical evidence to back up such an endeavor, for research shows that people who live in walkable, connected neighborhoods have lower rates of obesity, diabetes, high blood pressure, and heart disease (Grauerholz 2016).

The WST is a partnership between private business and not-for-profits. Concerning environmental and wellness standards, the key figure is Paul

Scialla, founder and CEO of Delos, the company that pioneered Wellness Real Estate and WELL. He launched the International WELL Building Institute in 2013 after pledging to share WELL globally in the CGI Commitment to Action. It is a public benefit corporation committed to balancing profitability with public benefits. Beside assuming that the project's individual buildings meet WELL certification, the intent is that each building will attain Leadership in Energy and Environmental Design certification (Grauerholz 2016).

The WST is a case that shows how wellness real estate relates to commercial services and urban amenities. It also contributes to the symbolic capital of the city. As said by Bob Buckhorn, the mayor of Tampa, sustainability and health polish the city's image, and demonstrates in a very concrete way that urban design can promote health and sustainability, making Tampa a model city in the field of wellness-oriented urban revitalization (Grauerholz 2016).

Attracting Tourists to Health and Wellness Destinations

As the locality as a dissipative structure interacts with its economic environment, its strategic locality development should be planned and designed with such a fundamental condition in mind (Anttiroiko 2015). Such an approach operates at several levels. At the level of regions or metropolitan areas the primary focus is on regional infrastructures and intermunicipal synergies. At the city level urban amenities, logistics, and livability are important issues. At the inner city or neighborhood level the development aim is primarily to create lively, attractive, and pleasant environments. Areas with special functions, such as technopolises, special economic zones, and industrial districts are designed to be attractive to business, whereas business improvement districts, wellness retail areas, and wellness quarters intend to attract consumers. As emphasized by Blakely and Bradshaw (2002, 181), *land use planning* is not only about maps, regulations, or zoning, but should also serve attraction and image management and thus pay attention to the sense of place, livability, protection of sensitive land areas, and the attractiveness of the city center, with mixed spaces that serve local business, consumption, and residents' quality of life.

In this section, our focus is on demand-driven, urban economic development strategies with wellness as their thematic core. This family of wellness city projects relies primarily on medical, health, and wellness tourism, destination development, and flagship facilities, such as large-scale spas, fitness centers, and health care complexes. In terms of governance, such projects represent different approaches to wellness city development, from purely private, to partnership-based, to public.

Good examples of such endeavors include large-scale wellness destinations and resorts, such as Mines Wellness City in Malaysia, and demand-driven health care or multi-function destinations, such as Dubai Healthcare City in UAE or Jeju Healthcare Town in Jeju island, South Korea. Before a closer look at these cases, let us discuss briefly their common denominator, i.e. medical and wellness tourism.

Medical and Wellness Tourism

Consuming inhabitants and tourists represent two heterogeneous groups with different roles in cities as dissipative structures. Inhabitants are sources of local consumption and tourists come from outside the locality to use services provided by local destinations, or just to experience the city itself. The latter are essential in economic development, for they generate income in the community and help it to grow. It requires tourism promotion to which thousands of local communities and tourism destinations have committed themselves in different parts of the world.

Medical tourism dates back to ancient times, when temples and temple spas served as health centers that provided cures for illnesses, and when hot and mineral springs attracted visitors from afar due to their assumed health benefits. Their influence continued through the centuries, as when the European elite rediscovered Roman baths and traveled to renowned spa towns. In early modern times, aristocrats especially traveled a lot for health purposes to places blessed with a healthy climate, or to local spas or health retreats. Until the early decades of the twentieth century, medical travels were primarily limited to the affluent who traveled to other countries to receive high-end medical services, especially in Europe and the USA. This situation soon changed and the international medical tourism market started to expand due to increased costs in developed countries, better offshore services, and emerging trends, such as new forms of pilgrimage and spiritual travels, which contributed to the rediscovery of Asian traditional thinking and medicine. Healthcare facilities in Asia started to attract Western visitors in the 1990s, as did those in Latin America for health travelers from the USA. Medical travel covered a wide range of health and wellness motivations, everything from facelifts, to bypass surgery, to fertility treatments (Health-tourism.com 2017). In all, *medical tourism* became a special segment of tourism, including all the relationships and phenomena resulting from a journey and residence by people whose main motive is to preserve or promote their health and overall well-being (cf. Mueller and Lanz Kaufmann 2000). A characteristic feature of this market is—and has been since its beginnings—the intertwining of health care and hospitality (DeMicco 2017).

Tourists buy local products and services while traveling, which makes them common targets in local economic development. They increasingly seek wellness services, facilities, and experiences from their travels, which usually flow from developed countries to less developed ones (Smith and Kelly 2006). This became a new mode of health, medical, or wellness tourism, the terminological choice depending roughly on whether the emphasis is on overall health promotion, medical treatments, or leisure and relaxation in spas, baths, or other wellness destinations (cf. Erfurt-Cooper and Cooper 2009). What is common to all of these terms is the desire to seek actively enhanced health and well-being. Even if medical tourism has become a prevalent term in this research field, it is rather narrow as it only covers the medical side of the health continuum (Global Wellness Institute 2015; on health and wellness tourism, see Smith and Puczkó 2009). Medical tourism implies that medical treatment or an improvement in a physical condition is the main motivation for a trip. A large part of the health tourism market is medical or health care tourism, which combines tourism with modern health care. Genuine *wellness tourism*, however, implies a search for lifestyle-related physical, mental, emotional, or spiritual well-being (cf. Smith and Kelly 2006). It brings spas, fitness, meditation, spirituality, and alternative medicine into the picture. Wellness tourism, with its peculiarities, makes it look actually somewhat esoteric or occasionally even weird. Besides, there is not always empirical evidence of the benefit of wellness treatments, which can make it a target of skepticism or open criticism (Smith and Kelly 2006). This situation is slowly changing as consumers, businesses, and governments seek an evidence-based approach to wellness.

What is the factual role of, say, mineral water or mud therapy, healthy diet, or meditation for improving our health? There is increasing evidence that in many cases wellness therapies and lifestyle changes have a positive impact on health (see e.g. Fraioli et al. 2011; see the website of the Wellness Evidence at http://www.wellnessevidence.com/wellnessevidence). It is also good to keep in mind that a large part of wellness is more about exercise, relaxation, and mindfulness than about cure or treatment. For many countries, this non-medical side of wellness tourism is extremely important. For example, well-being or wellness tourism in Finland emphasizes nature, peace and quiet, outdoor activities, and cultural offerings, including unique sauna experiences. Strategic wellness tourism offerings in the country not only include a few conventional spas, such as Naantali Spa, but also more exotic travel packages, especially in Lapland, such as the Arctic Aihki wilderness retreat in Salla, a Folk Healers' Gathering around mid-July in Kuusamo, Sauna Tour in Kuusamo, and a White Adventure silence and nature tour in Lapland (Visit Finland 2016).

Medical and wellness tourism rides a wave of global demographic and lifestyle changes that have been discussed earlier in this book. The area of broadly defined Wellness+ tourism is vast, and we can say without exaggeration that the amount it makes is huge, globally in 2015 that was about USD 560 billion in all, which accounts for some 15% of all tourism expenditure. It provides business opportunities along the vast health continuum, making it possible to utilize local strengths regarding the choice of target markets, specialization, and product differentiation. It is worth emphasizing that domestic wellness tourism is considerably larger than international. The former may be leveraged to attract international medical and wellness tourists, who consume more than the average international tourist. Wellness offerings also serve to differentiate destinations as people seek authentic, locally rooted experiences (Global Wellness Institute 2015). This has made wellness tourism appealing to local governments and development agencies and has led to the mushrooming of health and wellness destinations (Dvorak et al. 2014). Let us next take a brief look at some examples of destinations that are purposefully designed responses to growing international medical and wellness tourism.

Attraction Through Wellness Resort: Mines Wellness City

Mines Wellness City (MWC), formerly known as Mines Resort City, is an integrated health and wellness resort township in Seri Kembangan in the state of Selangor, only some 15 minutes' drive from Kuala Lumpur, the capital of Malaysia. The site was formerly a large open-cast tin mine. The deserted mining pit was once considered unviable for any form of construction. However, in the late 1980s the government of Malaysia designated this vast area for recreational and touristic purposes, entrusting it to

Country Heights, with Tan Sri Dato' Paduka Lee Kim Yew at the helm, who soon after turned the mining pit into a lake. Restoring large masses of land and then building around the lake, the property was designed to become Malaysia's first integrated health and wellness resort. The initial resort plan was completed by the end of the 1990s. It soon expanded and the functionality and brand of the area transformed, including its new name, Mines Wellness City, with a status of mega-project supported by Malaysia's Economic Transformation Program (ETP). The ETP was actually an important framework for the project as a government initiative introduced in 2010 with the aim of turning Malaysia into a high-income economy by 2020. One of the key national economic areas included in the plan was private health care, with MWC as its flagship project (Mines Wellness City 2014).

MWC is an embodiment of the corporate philosophy of its master developer, Country Heights Holdings Berhad. A fundamental idea was to stress the importance of preventive health care and a balanced lifestyle that contributes to building healthy communities, which are imperatives in today's stressful and fast-paced world. The area itself witnessed a rapid transformation after the 1990s, with many flagship facilities:

- A luxury hotel, Palace of the Golden Horses;
- Mines Wellness Hotel with man-made beach and swimming lagoon;
- Golden Horses Health Sanctuary;
- The Mines shopping mall;
- Mines Waterfront Business Park;
- Mines Resort and Golf Club;
- Mines Convention Centre; and
- The Heritage—office tower, residences, village, and hotel.

The most prominent facility for the health care and wellness services of the area is the Golden Horses Health Sanctuary, which fulfills the Malaysian Government's emphasis on preventive health care. What is characteristic of the center is that under the same roof there are both Western scientific detection technologies and Eastern natural treatment (ENT) therapies. Thus, beside early detection (health screening and genetic screening) and preventive care (a heart clinic, ENT specialist, health and dietetic clinic, and allergy and food intolerance) there is a center that offers traditional Chinese medicine therapies, Qi Gong, and a herbal medicine dispensary (see http://www.ghhs.com.my/).

As a large-scale integrated health and wellness destination, MWC plays a significant role in local economic development. It not only utilizes the global wellness tourism trend but also localizes it through considerable investment and by creating business and job opportunities for nearby communities. It promotes wider integration with the first, second, and third places of the community (i.e. home, work, and public places) to promote conscious living and holistic health (Mines Wellness City 2014). The elements of a sustainable city have become integral to the development of the MWC, for it is to become eco-friendly and support organic and negative ion living.

The MWC attracts developers and service operators with considerable tax exemptions. It provides various ways of participating in the development of the area for investors. As a special economic development area with a wellness focus there is a list of qualifying activities, ranging from hospitals, clinics, and nursing homes, to traditional medicine, health care and wellness education, spa, and healthy food. Moreover, as always with these kinds of destination, what ultimately makes the area viable is its appeal to domestic and international tourists who through their consumption generate income and economic growth.

Wellness Zoning as Attraction Strategy: Dubai Healthcare City

Dubai in the United Arab Emirates is a unique, globally oriented, consumption driven economy, in which the autocratic regime, led by the ruler of the city-state, dedicated its oil wealth to building a themed economy that attracts globally advanced services, facilities, and both high-end and mass tourism. Its development extensively utilizes special economic zones and large-scale destinations, as illustrated by such developments as Dubai Healthcare City, Dubai Sports City, Children's City, and Dubai Knowledge Village (see Schmid 2009; Bagaeen 2007; Anttiroiko 2015).

Dubai Healthcare City (DHCC) is a health care free economic zone launched in 2002 by the ruler of Dubai, Sheikh Mohammed Bin Rashid Al Maktoum. It was mandated by the government to meet the demand for high-quality, patient-centered health care with an aim to attract wealthy tourists to the city. Beside health care it provides medical education and research, pharmaceuticals, medical equipment, and wellness services. Phase 1 of the DHCC focuses on health care and medical education in Oud Metha, while Phase 2 is dedicated to wellness in Al Jadaf. The city became operational in the early 2010s (Reisman 2010).

DHCC attracts more than a million visitors yearly, of which some one-fifth are international medical tourists, seeking infertility, cosmetic, and dental treatments. It plays an important role in the regional economy, for the Gulf area had lost medical tourists to overseas destinations, especially to Asia. Such a situation started to attract the attention of the governments of the region. Dubai was one of the most ambitious and diligent on that front and after the launch of DHCC became a major destination in the area (Connell 2011, 55). It has some 1.8 billion potential patients within a four-hour flight (Reisman 2010, 169). DHCC's primary customer base is in the Gulf area and the Middle East, while a slightly smaller share of customers are from elsewhere in Asia and from Europe. In DHCC's marketing new target markets include medical tourists from China, Russia, and East Africa (see https://www.dhcc.ae/; on the use of the services of DHCC, see Woodman 2012).

DHCC is a free economic zone committed to creating a health and wellness destination, overseen by the Dubai Healthcare City Authority and regulated by its independent regulatory arm, whose quality standards are accredited by the International Society for Quality in Healthcare. It has systematically built its reputation as an internationally recognized location of quality health care and an integrated center of excellence for clinical and wellness services, medical education, and research. One way of increasing its credibility, expertise, and appeal has been to recruit doctors from Western countries and to apply Western quality standards, as has been done in many other health care hubs in the Middle East. DHCC has westernized the brands of many local private health care providers by labeling them with country names generally associated with high-quality medicine, as in Canadian Specialist Hospital and American Hospital Dubai. The latter is a member of the Mayo Clinic Care Network, which in turn utilizes the world-class brand of the Rochester-based Mayo Clinic (Madson 2016; Nisen 2013). DHCC also has a connection with Harvard Medical International, a global arm of Harvard Medical School. All these serve a strategic purpose of attracting the best expertise and renowned health care brands to Dubai, which contribute to the city-state's ability to attract wealthy medical tourists. Beside quality and reputation, economic factors also have a role to play. Dubai has been able to provide quality treatment at lower prices than in the USA or the UK, though it is generally considered to be more expensive than India or Thailand (Reisman 2010; Connell 2011).

DHCC has close to 160 clinical partners, including hospitals, outpatient medical centers, and diagnostic laboratories, across a wide range of specialties, with licensed professionals from several countries. It is also home to the Mohammed Bin Rashid University of Medicine and Health Sciences. In addition, there are close to 200 retail and non-clinical facilities serving the area (see https://www.dhcc.ae/). In all, it is a multi-cultural health destination created and promoted by a developmental state, which, as one of the most successful attraction economies of our time, has been able to deal with the challenges of an increasingly fluid global economy.

Medical Service Business District: Jeju Healthcare Town

Metropolitan areas and regions depend on their position in the national political-administrative structure as well as on their strengths and weaknesses in the global competition between cities. Even if cities have some competitive advantages in health and wellness industries, in a competitive environment it may not be that easy to reclaim such an advantage. Jeju island in South Korea provides an interesting case in this respect.

Jeju is an island south of the Korean peninsula. It is a fairly remote location from a Korean point of view, not least because most of the power, population growth, and economic life concentrates on the Seoul metropolitan area. Considering its geographical position, Jeju has some advantages, for it is only a one-hour flight from Seoul and a two-hour flight from 18 Asian cities, most of them having several million inhabitants, including Beijing, Shanghai, Tianjin, Hong Kong, and Tokyo (Stephano and Abratt 2012).

Jeju is administratively an autonomous province, with considerable leeway in its economic development. The state-owned company Jeju Free International City Development Center (JDC) was established under the Ministry of Land, Transport and Maritime Affairs. In recent decades, it has worked for six flagship projects: Jeju Global Education City, Jeju Science Park, Resort-type Residential Complex, Myths and History Theme Park, Seogwipo Tourism Port, and Jeju Healthcare Town (JHT). Concerning the last one, in the early 2000s JDC unveiled plans for "Healthcare Town," which aimed at making Jeju a resort-style medical tourism destination. Its initial price tag was approximately USD 315 million, which later rose considerably after the inclusion of international investors. JDC planned to attract medical travelers by merging Jeju's clean and green natural environment, surrounded by the sea, with cutting-edge health care, from medical examinations and obesity treatments to wellness therapies (Stephano and Abratt 2012).

The healthcare town plan was a response to the fact that the medical tourism market had been growing fast, both in Korea and internationally. In 2009, some 60,201 travelers visited Korea for medical treatments in dermatology, plastic surgery, and gynecology, bringing some KRW 54.7 billion income to the country, while in the following year the number of medical tourists increased by 36% to 81,789, and almost doubled the profits from the previous year. Of these tourists, 32% were Americans, some 20% were Chinese, and 17% were Japanese. In the 2010s, Jeju saw a significant rise in Chinese tourists, encouraged by visa-free access to the island. In 2014 some four million Chinese tourists visited Korea, of which 1.8 million came to Jeju, which increased local developers' interest in this particular consumer segment. For the same reason, Jeju attracted the attention of investors beyond the Yellow Sea.

The JDC assumed that it would expand and develop the island's medical tourism market while developing it on an international level, which was supposed to boost the local economy. The JDC attempted to attract leading domestic and overseas medical institutions to the island and create a special medical zone as part of its efforts to establish an advanced health care infrastructure befitting an international free city (Stephano and Abratt 2012). The timeline of JHT was (JDC n/a):

2008 Urban management plan finalized
2009 Development project implementation approved
2010 Ownership transfer of business site completed
2011 Site construction started
2012 Construction phase 1 of Greenland Group completed
2013 Memorandum of understanding (MOU) between JDC-Seoul National University Hospital and Greenland Group signed
2014 Construction phase 2 of Greenland Group started (Healing Spiral Hotel Building) and MOU with JDC-Greenland Group for further investment signed
2015 The establishment of foreign medical institutions approved by the Ministry of Health and Welfare (Greenland International Hospital); and Designation of the Greenland Group as a Foreign Investment Zone announced
2016 Site construction completed; and MOU with JDC-Korea Health Industry Development Institute signed to activate medical tourism in Jeju Healthcare Town.

The JHT had its groundbreaking ceremony in Seogwipo city in 2012 after JDC signed an MOU with the Greenland Group, which promised to invest KRW 1 trillion to implement the JHT project. The first phase was built in Donghong-dong and Topyeong-dong areas some five kilometers from Seogwipo city center, and was completed in 2016. The resort and medical service complex has three sites, each serving a special function: Medical Park, Wellness Park, and R&D Park (Stephano and Abratt 2012).

- The Medical Park is a center that provides treatment for specialties like cancer, cardiovascular issues, vascular disease, and spine problems. It includes a professional hospital complex providing professional and specialized medical services; a retirement community with retirement and medical research activities; and a town for older people requiring long-term care (JDC n/a).
- The Wellness Park provides general health improvement services, including check-ups, beauty treatments, and oriental medicine, as well as various lodging facilities. It includes a recreational resort for leading happy lives through physical and mental health care; various programs for preventive treatment, health care, and health promotion; and facilities to enjoy exercise and recreation, such as outdoor areas and indoor recreation spaces (JDC n/a).
- The R&D Park will focus on research, particularly in geriatrics. It has been planned to include clinical research centers and new drug development research centers, such as the Medical R&D Center and Anti-Aging Center for developing technology and products in the medical service field (JDC n/a).

JHT includes medical and research facilities, foreign medical facilities, shopping malls, accommodation facilities, and recreational cultural facilities. As the island had already developed as a tourist hub, it offers visitors many other attractions, such as: the world's largest botanical garden, Bunjae Artpia; the country's tallest mountain, Halla-San; the Dragon's Head Rock along the coast; the Samseonghyeol holes in downtown Jeju city; and the Hallasan National Park (Stephano and Abratt 2012).

International collaboration has become an important part of promoting JHT. One of the key private players in pushing the project further has been the Greenland Group, based in Shanghai, China, which invested close to USD 1 billion to the Jeju project. JDC provides administrative, PR, and marketing support in taking the project forward (Stephano and Abratt 2012). From the point of view of Korean investors, Jeju may not have been a first priority, especially when thinking of the appeal of high-tech developments and real estate businesses on the mainland and in the capital region in particular. Thus, JHT had to seek foreign investments and partnerships, which it eventually found from China and the United Arab Emirates. A few Chinese real estate firms started to invest in the health care project, which gave it a new lease of life. This relationship was boosted because Jeju has been a popular destination for Chinese tourists for some time. In addition, the Ministry of Health and Welfare signed an agreement with the Abu Dhabi Health Authority in the UAE in 2011 to help Korea's medical institutions attract patients. This alliance was expected to help attract medical tourists from the Middle East to Jeju, partially because Abu Dhabi has had a practice of providing public funds to some 3000 patients every year to seek treatment overseas. Lastly, JDC struck up a partnership with the Hospital for Sick Children in Toronto, Canada. Through a MOU, the two agreed to work together on exchanges, and JDC was supposed to adapt the hospital's operating system and know-how with respect to pediatrics (Stephano and Abratt 2012).

While attracting both foreign investments and medical tourists is generally a good thing in terms of jobs and economic growth, the presence of Chinese investors has also increased concerns among local residents, especially because in the first half of the 2010s the land area purchased by the Chinese increased dramatically. One of the concerns was that while Chinese landowners purchased the land mainly with tourism in mind, some local critics would have preferred to see more emphasis put on manufacturing and technology co-operation between China and Korea in the development of the regional economy. The provincial government has acknowledged this message and come up with a plan to diversify the inflow of foreign investments by including a broad set of countries and widening the variety of investment projects (Arirang News 2013). Another concern has been the commercialization of health care, especially after the approval of the first for-profit hospital, the Greenland International Hospital, by the Ministry of Health and Welfare in 2015 (Huh 2015). It opened in 2017 with an initial mission to focus on Chinese tourists visiting Jeju for plastic surgery and skin treatment. Lastly, the political economy of tourism is rather fragile in the region, especially after the Chinese government pressured travel agencies not to sell travel packages to Korea and discouraged Chinese citizens from visiting Korea due to its objections to South Korea's deployment of the THAAD missile defense system (Gibson 2017). Such issues have pushed forward the provincial government's general aim of diversifying the regional economy, among the new trends being to support the livelihoods of residents and a carbon-free future by promoting the preservation of the environment, promoting the use of renewable energy, and the uptake of electric vehicles (Yamada 2017).

Innovative, Export-Driven Wellness Cities

An important part of wellness city development can be based on export promotion that relies on scientific research and technological innovations, having its industrial core in biomedical, biotechnology, pharmaceutical, and medical device industries. Such wellness city endeavors revolve around knowledge, innovation, and smartness applied to technological, medical, and professional aspects of health and wellness.

This section offers a brief discussion of a few cases that represent different faces of health care industries and technology-driven urban health care and wellness. The role of universities and industrial health and wellness clusters is briefly discussed with reference to the cities of Sendai, Japan, and Austin, Texas. Wellness-focused business parks, incubators, and accelerators are slowly increasing, of which a good example is our last case, Healthcare City in Lisbon.

The Rise of Industrial, Innovation, and Service Districts

Discussion about industrial districts has long roots that take us back to the late nineteenth century and the writings of Alfred Marshall (1890/1920). *Industrial district*refers to an area where a concentration of firms has settled down. It may start as a simple co-location of small firms, which over time becomes a more "compound" localization, that is, an industrial district, with a special atmosphere, close connections, shared information, and a specialization that gives advantages to firms gathered together in a particular area (Belussi and Caldari 2009; Becattini 2004). In the case of the cluster of same-sector businesses and employees deriving benefits from their geographical proximity we speak of *localization economies*, whereas in highly urbanized areas where there are many industry groups together with a complex array of economic and social institutions, *agglomeration economies* emerge, or as they are sometimes called, *urbanization economies* (Badcock 2014). Such formations are today much more diverse than original industrial districts, including hub-and-spoke industrial districts and government-sponsored areas, and later post-Fordist manufacturing zones with their reliance on flexible production systems (Badcock 2014).

Concerning manufacturing, basic, and applied research, and corporate R&D, there are several geographical concentrations, some being more industrial, some more research-oriented. The most archetypal forms of industrial district are *medical and biotechnological industrial districts*, such as Shanghai Chemical Industry Park in China or Tuas Biomedical Park in Singapore. Many multi-function biotechnology parks have evolved from biotech or pharmaceutical industries, such as Philadelphia's biotechnology district, and have usually developed towards a science park model (Llobrera et al. 2000). Indeed, biotechnology and related industries are highly dependent on new ideas and basic research conducted in leading academic institutions, research centers, and laboratories. That is why most such concentrations are *medical or biotech science parks* that, beside industrial corporations, host universities and R&D institutes, as in the cases of the Biomedical Discovery District on the University of Minnesota's Twin Cities campus in Minneapolis, or the UMass Medicine Science Park in Worcester, Massachussets (see McKelvey et al. 2004). Other examples of biotech parks, districts, valleys, and clusters are such European sites as: LISAvienna, Austria's largest life sciences district (http://lisavienna.at); BioWin health cluster in Wallonia, Belgium (http://www.biowin.org); the Danish-Swedish life science cluster Medicon Valley centering around Greater Copenhagen (see Medicon Valley Alliance at http://mva.org); Tartu Biotechnology Park in Estonia (http://biopark.ee); Uppsala BIO in Sweden (https://www.uppsalabio.com); Lyonbiopole, a bio cluster that promotes innovation in health care and life sciences in the Auvergne-Rhône-Alpes region, France (https://lyonbiopole.com); and Leiden Bio Science Park in the Netherlands (https://leidenbiosciencepark.nl). There are also many smaller-scale incubators and accelerators in this field, such as MediCity and BioCity in Nottingham, the latter being one of the first biotech incubators in the UK (http://www.biocity.co.uk/biocity/nottingham), and Healthcare City with its main premises in Taguspark, Oeiras, Greater Lisbon, Portugal (http://healthcarecity.pt).

Beside sites of production and innovation, there are also *service districts or complexes*, which attract consumption. Medical and hospital districts emerged in the twentieth century as concentrations of public and/or private hospitals and clinics to serve their customers. Such service complexes include the major hospital sites of regional hospital districts, public-private or purely private medical districts, medical tourist destinations, and multi-function wellness districts. For example, Medical District northwest of downtown Dallas has the University of Texas Southwestern Medical Center campus as its anchor. Another example is the Medical District in the Near Southside, south of downtown Fort Worth, Texas, which is home to Tarrant County's major hospitals and many independent medical clinics (Near Southside, Inc. n/a).

Health and Welfare Cluster in Sendai

Health and wellness technologies form a significant industry in many metropolises in the USA, Europe, and East Asia. They form a base on which to build one of the most appealing options of wellness cluster developments, which, at the intersection of technological development and expanding health and wellness clusters, can benefit from productivity growth, innovation intensity, and high value-added activities, and thus become a viable part of the local economy.

Japan has developed world-class technological capacities, and utilizes it in local and regional economic development. For instance, Tokyo has a huge concentration of expertise and resources in this field. A special creation some 50 kilometers northeast of Tokyo is Tsukuba Science City, a unique concentration of government, corporate, and university research institutes, which has considerable strengths in medical research, biotechnology, and life sciences. Another world-class concentration is in Kansai area, including Osaka, Kyoto, and Kobe, with considerable strengths in biotechnology and pharmaceuticals. It is particularly strong in life sciences and biotechnology, including drug discovery, medical technology, in vitro diagnostics, medical devices and equipment, and functional foodstuffs (see http://www.biobridge-kansai.com/). There are also a number of other cities around the country, with special strengths in health and wellness industries; one example being the university city of Sendai.

Sendai is the center of Tohoku region, north of Tokyo, with some one million inhabitants. It has a reputation as a pleasant and prosperous academic city with a particular strength in educating industrial human resources. It strongly promotes policies to attract research-oriented businesses to the region. The city has ten universities and several other educational institutions. Primus inter pares is Tohoku University as the third imperial university of the country (Nature.com 2006). Sendai has surged to the wellness business through its pioneering science, produced especially in Tohoku University.

Tohoku University is known for its entrepreneurial efforts and close business–academia collaboration. Sendai's target industries attracted to the Special Zone for Promoting Private Investment include a wide variety of high-tech industries, among them medical and health-related industries. An indication of Sendai's focus on the development of a health care and welfare cluster is the establishment of a flagship facility, The Sendai Finland Wellbeing Center (Sendai FWBC), which is the core for a growing agglomeration of IT and service companies in the health and welfare sectors. Its main function is to support manufacturers and service providers to develop products and services in the nursing care field (see http://sendai.fwbc.jp/en/index.html).

The Sendai FWBC offers incubation facilities to support the commercialization of health care and welfare-related devices and services. It has also a special nursing home designed in a Finnish style. Companies and universities in Finland and Sendai are working together to support the internationalization of health care and welfare-related industries. The center is also engaged in supporting IT companies to enter health care markets, including such new areas as games and mobile applications (JETRO 2017).

Merging Technology with Health Care in Austin

As a rising US high-tech city, Austin, the capital of Texas, has become a name that many other cities envy, one of its nicknames being Silicon Hills. Even if it does not match New York or San Francisco in many respects, it has gained a reputation as an American startup mecca (Pofeldt 2016), and a place of cool urban culture, "a city that's increasingly comfortable just being itself" (Hensel 2017). Austin is one of the most attractive cities in the high-tech field with a young, educated population, a renowned high-tech community, and the presence of venture capitalists. This appeal is further increased by reasonable real estate prices, a revitalized downtown, and the extra incentive of a city government that does not levy personal income tax. Lastly, it is not an insignificant factor that Greater Austin is the home of multinational computer technology company Dell.

In 2011 Senator Kirk Watson of Austin introduced the long-term plan known as 10 Goals in 10 Years to transform the health and economy of Austin and Travis County. Essential components of this plan included fostering health care innovation and research. Actually, one of the major deficiencies of the University of Texas and the whole city was the lack of a medical school and teaching hospital. After the plan was accepted, the Dell Medical School at the University of Texas and a modern teaching and safety-net hospital, Dell Seton Medical Center at the University of Texas, were established. After these developments the next step was to encourage Austin's high-tech industries to create synergies with health care (Bohigian 2016).

Dell is an important part of the story of Austin's efforts to seek leadership in the health technology industry. Namely, with the creation of the Dell Medical School and Dell Seton Medical Center, located in the center of the city, Austin is rapidly increasing its reputation as a health care hub. Beside medical school and health centers, there are over 200 life science companies within a 25-mile radius of downtown Austin.

Austin has been strengthening its innovation capacity for years. One of the fairly recent moves was the establishment of the Innovation Zone Working Group that put special efforts into learning how to stimulate innovation, creativity, and economic activity. Its work led to the creation of Capital City Innovation Inc., a non-profit with a mission to facilitate the innovation zone and ensure broad community benefit (Bohigian 2016). Its job is to help established businesses and enterprising startups become part of the health ecosystem that is developing around the Dell Medical School and a new teaching hospital. The geographical concentration of activities is named as an Innovation Zone, anchored on the University of Texas. At the heart of this zone sits the 14.3-acre Central Health Brackenridge Campus, which is located immediately south of the medical school and teaching hospital.

In Austin, developers have paid attention to the same phenomenon that has started to attract the attention of urban developers throughout the developed world during the last few years. At the intersection of the thriving technology industry and the burgeoning health care industry there is an excellent opportunity for creating businesses and well-paid jobs. An area where this intersection manifests itself is digital health, that is, medical devices, health care applications, and consumer products that can help Austin build a more diverse, data-driven health care model, one that addresses both services and health care delivery. This is just the tip of the iceberg when it comes to the opportunities for health technology development (Bohigian 2016).

Health Care Business Incubator in Lisbon

The Healthcare City by the Nova Medical School in Lisbon, Portugal, is one of the pioneers in focused health care business incubation. It has special features as an incubator, including its affiliation with a medical school, the central role given to founder companies, ecosystem thinking, and global orientation. The Healthcare City is headquartered in Lisbon, with premises in Taguspark in Oeiras, a neighboring city to Lisbon. It was launched in April 2016. During the first seven months, it received over 150 applications from 11 countries, and by the end of the year it had started to work with more than ten startups (Hagan 2016). The incubator aims to support 250 entrepreneurs in the first three years, providing them with sufficient services, mentoring, office space, and access to labs and hospitals for piloting. The program targets not only startups but also small companies seeking growth.

In other markets innovation can take shortcuts, but in health care innovative ideas take a long and winding road to reach markets. High R&D intensity, special funding needs, a regulated business environment, and a high dependence on distribution networks are some of the challenges faced by health care entrepreneurs. The entire ecosystem gathered around the Healthcare City is utilized to deal with such sector-specific challenges. One of the key tasks is to attract investors who understand the need for a long validation cycle that takes years, sometimes more than a decade.

The Healthcare City was created to increase the survival rate of new businesses and to place the capital of Portugal on the health care innovation map. It resulted from a partnership between NOVA Medical School, the Janssen Pharmaceutical Companies of Johnson & Johnson, health insurer Medis of the Ocidental Group, and Portuguese healthcare provider Lusíadas Saúde Group of AMIL and UnitedHealth, which together represent academia and various aspects of health care businesses, to give the incubated initiatives holistic support and help them to reach the market (Norões 2016).

Healthcare City has an ambitious goal to help startups launch their products or services on the global market. For this, the startups can rely on the support of the multi-disciplinary operational team of the incubator, with people with backgrounds ranging from business to medicine and biology, as well as on the network of mentors and founders. By having the industry within the incubator, startups have support for market testing and even selling their products through the founding companies' distribution and sales structures. This is a characteristic feature of the Healthcare City: it is not only the first of its kind in Portugal, specialized in health care and well-being, but it is based on the active involvement of industrial partners.

References

Angelidou, M. (2015). Smart Cities: A Conjuncture of Four Forces. *Cities, 47*, 95–106.

Anttiroiko, A.-V. (2015). *New Urban Management: Attracting Value Flows to Branded Hubs*. Basingstoke: Palgrave Macmillan.

Anttiroiko, A.-V. (2016). City-as-a-Platform: The Rise of Participatory Innovation Platforms in Finnish Cities. *Sustainability, 8*(9), Article 922.

Anttiroiko, A.-V., & Valkama, P. (2016). Post-NPM-Style Service Integration: Partnership-Based Brokerage in Elderly Care. *International Journal of Public Sector Management, 29*(7), 675–689.

Anttiroiko, A.-V., Valkama, P., & Bailey, S. J. (2013). Smart Cities in the New Service Economy: Building Platforms for Smart Services. *AI & Society, 29*, 323–334.

Arirang News. (2013). *Chinese Investors Flock to Jeju*. Report by Yoo Li-an, Arirang News, Jeju, in YouTube. Retrieved September 9, 2017, from https://www.youtube.com/watch?v=ia_K24nUo7I

Badcock, B. (2014). *Making Sense of Cities: A Geographical Survey*. London/New York: Routledge.

Bagaeen, S. (2007). Brand Dubai: The Instant City; or the Instantly Recognizable City. *International Planning Studies, 12*(2), 173–197.

Beaglehole, R., Bonita, R., Horton, R., Adams, O., & McKee, M. (2004). Public Health in the New Era: Improving Health Through Collective Action. *The Lancet, 363*, 2084–2086.

Becattini, G. (2004). *Industrial Districts: A New Approach to Industrial Change*. Cheltenham: Edward Elgar.

Belussi, F., & Caldari, K. (2009). At the Origin of the Industrial District: Alfred Marshall and the Cambridge School. *Cambridge Journal of Economics, 33*, 335–355.

Bhargava, K., & Bhargava, D. (2007). Evidence Based Health Care: A Scientific Approach to Health Care. *Sultan Qaboos University Medical Journal, 7*(2), 105–107.

Bhatt, C., Dey, N., & Ashour, A. (Eds.). (2017). *Internet of Things and Big Data Technologies for Next Generation Healthcare*. Basel: Springer International Publishing.

Blakely, E. J., & Bradshaw, T. K. (2002). *Planning Local Economic Development: Theory and Practice* (3rd ed.). Thousand Oaks: Sage.

Bohigian, A. (2016, November 1). The Austin Healthcare Innovation Zone: Where Tech and Healthcare Merge. *Enolabs* (Blog). Retrieved September 3, 2017, from https://www.enolalabs.com/blog/archives/the-austin-healthcare-innovation-zone-where-tech-and-healthcare-merge

Burton, D., & Haughom, J. (n/a). What Is an Accountable Care Organization (ACO)? *Health Catalyst*. Retrieved September 3, 2017, from https://www.healthcatalyst.com/what-is-an-ACO-definitive-guide-accountable-care-organizations

Connell, J. (2011). *Medical Tourism*. Wallingford: CAB International.

DeMicco, F. J. (Ed.). (2017). *Medical Tourism and Wellness: Hospitality Bridging Healthcare (H2H)*. Oakville: Apple Academic Press.

Dvorak, D., Saari, S., & Tuominen, T. (Eds.). (2014). *Developing a Competitive Health and Well-Being Destination*. Turku: Turku University of Applied Sciences.

Ellis, J., & Razavi, A. (2012, September 14). Healthcare Innovation Zone—Challenging Providers to Improve Care. *Healthcare Finance*. Retrieved September 3, 2017, from http://www.healthcarefinancenews.com/blog/healthcare-innovation-zone-challenging-providers-improve-care

EPA. (2012, December). *Smart Growth and Economic Success: Benefits for Real Estate Developers, Investors, Businesses, and Local Governments*. EPA's Office of Sustainable Communities. United States Environmental Protection Agency. Retrieved September 10, 2017, from https://www.epa.gov/sites/production/files/documents/smart_growth_and_economic_success.pdf

Erfurt-Cooper, P., & Cooper, M. (2009). *Health and Wellness Tourism: Spas and Hot Springs*. Bristol: Channel View Publications.

Fraioli, A., Serio, A., Mennuni, G., Ceccarelli, F., Petraccia, L., Fontana, M., Grassi, M., & Valesini, G. (2011). A Study on the Efficacy of Treatment with Mud Packs and Baths with Sillene Mineral Water (Chianciano Spa Italy) in Patients Suffering from Knee Osteoarthritis. *Rheumatology International, 31*(10), 1333–1340.

Gibson, J. (2017, March 23). China's Tourist Boycott Backfires on South Korea's Jeju Island. *The Diplomat*. Retrieved September 9, 2017, from http://thediplomat.com/2017/03/chinas-tourist-boycott-backfires-on-south-koreas-jeju-island/

Global Wellness Institute. (2015). *The Global Wellness Tourism Economy 2013 & 2014*. Miami: Global Wellness Institute.

Global Wellness Institute. (2016a). *Wellness Communities Initiative Resources* (Website). Miami: The Global Wellness Institute. Retrived September 9, 2017, from https://www.globalwellnessinstitute.org/wellness-communities-resources

Global Wellness Institute. (2016b). *GWI Wellness Communities Initiative White Paper*. Global Wellness Communities Initiative. Last Updated: September 2016. Retrieved September 10, 2017, from https://static1.squarespace.com/static/54306a8ee4b07ea66ea32cc0/t/588a5847ebbd1a2ab766a9b2/1485461576482/GWI+Wellness+Communities_WhitePaper_September+2016+EditionPTproofedFINAL1252017.pdf

Global Wellness Institute. (2017, January 31). *Redefining What It Means to Live Well: Exploring Wellness Communities & Lifestyle Real Estate* (2017 Roundtable Report). New York. Retrieved September 9, 2017, from https://static1.squarespace.com/static/54306a8ee4b07ea66ea32cc0/t/58e66962b3db2b4c6025bebc/1491495271514/Wellness-Communities-and-Lifestyle-Real-Estate-Roundtable.pdf

Glushko, R. J. (2010). Seven Contexts for Service System Design. In P. P. Maglio, C. Kieliszewski, & J. Phohrer (Eds.), *Handbook of Service Science* (pp. 219–249). New York: Springer.

Grauerholz, M. (2016, January–February). Living Well: Tampa Becomes the First City in the World to Introduce a WELL Certified District. *USGBC+*. Retrieved August 28, 2017, from http://plus.usgbc.org/living-well/

Griffin, J. (2017, June 27). Finally, Jeff Vinik's Vision Has a Name: Water Street Tampa. *Tampa Bay Times*. Retrieved August 29, 2017, from http://www.tampabay.com/news/business/finally-jeff-viniks-vision-has-a-name-water-street-tampa/2328569

Hagan, H. (2016, December 13). Healthcare City—A Quality Startups Incubator in the Healthcare and Wellness Industry. *Euspert.com*. Retrieved August 31, 2017, from https://news.euspert.com/healthcare-city-a-quality-startups-incubator-in-the-healthcare-and-wellness-industry/

Healey, P. (1994). Urban Policy and Property Development: The Institutional Relations of Real-Estate Development in an Old Industrial Region. *Environment and Planning A, 26*, 177–198.

Health-tourism.com. (2017). *The History of Medical Tourism*. Retrieved August 14, 2017, from https://www.health-tourism.com/medical-tourism/history/

Hensel, A. (2017, March 9). Austin Has Some Advice for Cities Trying to Become the Next Silicon Valley. *Inc*. Retrieved September 5, 2017, from https://www.inc.com/anna-hensel/austin-isnt-going-to-be-the-next-silicon-valley-and-its-perfectly-fine-with-that.html

Huh, H.-J. (2015, December 19). First for-Profit Hospital Approved for Jeju Island. *The Hankyoreh*. Retrieved September 9, 2017, from http://english.hani.co.kr/arti/english_edition/e_national/722655.html

Jablow, M. (2017, August 22). Author David Ansell Exposes Inequality's Deadly Influence. *AAMC News*. Retrieved September 3, 2017, from https://news.aamc.org/diversity/article/inequality-deadly-influence/

JDC. (n/a). *Healthcare Town*. Jeju Free International City Development Center. Retrieved September 9, 2017, from https://english.jdcenter.com/business/medic/healthcare.cs

JETRO. (2017, January). *Sendai City. Industrial Cluster Information*. Japan External Trade Organization (JETRO). Retrieved September 5, 2017, from https://www.jetro.go.jp/en/invest/region/sendai-city/icinfo.html

Kasvio, A., & Anttiroiko, A.-V. (Eds.). (2005). *e-City: Analysing Efforts to Generate Local Dynamism in the City of Tampere*. Tampere: Tampere University Press.

Kenneally, J., Prendergast, D., Maccani, G., Donnellan, B., & Helfert, M. (2014). Sustainable Connected Cities: Vision and Blueprint Towards Managing IT for City Prosperity and Sustainability. In M. Helfert, B. Donnellan, J. Kenneally (Eds.), *Design Science: Perspectives from Europe. EDSS 2013*, Communications in Computer and Information Science (Vol. 447). Cham: Springer.

Komninos, N. (2015). *The Age of Intelligent Cities: Smart Environments and Innovation-for-All Strategies*. London/New York: Routledge.

Komninos, N. (2016). Smart Environments and Smart Growth: Connecting Innovation Strategies and Digital Growth Strategies. *International Journal of Knowledge-Based Development, 7*(3), 240–263.

Kresser, C. (2017). *Unconventional Medicine: Join the Revolution to Reinvent Healthcare, Reverse Chronic Disease, and Create a Practice You Love*. Austin: Lioncrest Publishing.

Kume, Y. (2017, June). *Let's Enjoy Walking for the Benefits of Better Health—Smart Wellness Point Project*. JFS (Newsletter No. 178). Retrieved August 28, 2017, from http://www.japanfs.org/en/news/archives/news_id035856.html

Lim, J., Yun, Y., Lee, S., Cho, Y., & Chae, H. (2013). Perspectives on Medical Services Integration Among Conventional Western, Traditional Korean, and Dual-Licensed Medical Doctors in Korea. *Evidence-Based Complementary and Alternative Medicine: eCAM*. https://doi.org/10.1155/2013/105413.

Llobrera, J. T., Meyer, D. R., & Nammacher, G. (2000). Trajectories of Industrial Districts: Impact of Strategic Intervention in Medical Districts. *Economic Geography, 76*, 68–98.

Madson, R. (2016, June 1). American Hospital Dubai Joins Mayo Clinic Care Network. *Mayo Clinic, News Network*. Retrieved September 7, 2017, from https://newsnetwork.mayoclinic.org/discussion/american-hospital-dubai-joins-mayo-clinic-care-network/

March, W. (2016, August 23). What Is a Wellness District? Vinik-Cascade Project in Downtown Tampa Promotes Healthy Lifestyle. *83 degrees*. Retrieved August 28, 2017, from http://www.83degreesmedia.com/features/wellnessdistrict-Tampa-Vinik-SPP-Delos-082316.aspx

Marshall, A. (1890/1920). *Principles of Economics*. London: Macmillan.

McKelvey, M., Rickne, A., & Laage-Hellman, J. (Eds.). (2004). *The Economic Dynamics of Modern Biotechnology*. Cheltenham: Edward Elgar.

Memon, M., Wagner, S. R., Pedersen, C. F., Beevi, F. H. A., & Hansen, F. O. (2014). Ambient Assisted Living Healthcare Frameworks, Platforms, Standards, and Quality Attributes. *Sensors* (Basel), *14*(3), 4312–4341.

midika-iot.jp. (n/a). *Challenge Project for Charging IoT Health Services with Incentives*. Ministry of Internal Affairs and Communications. Retrieved September 15, 2017, from http://www.midika-iot.jp/en/project/207

Mikusz, M. (2015). *Towards a Conceptual Framework for Cyber-Physical Systems from the Service-Dominant Logic Perspective*. Twenty-first Americas Conference on Information Systems, Puerto Rico. Retrieved February 24, 2017, from http://aisel.aisnet.org/cgi/viewcontent.cgi?article=1082&context=amcis2015

Mines Wellness City. (2014). *Mines Wellness City: Malaysia's Wellness Hub* (Website). Retrieved September 6, 2017, from http://mineswellnesscity.com/

Mueller, H., & Kaufmann, E. L. (2000). Wellness Tourism: Market Analysis of a Special Health Tourism Segment and Implications for the Hotel Industry. *Journal of Vacation Marketing*, *7*(1), 5–17.

Murgante, B., & Borruso, G. (2015). Smart Cities in a Smart World. In S. T. Rassia & P. M. Pardalos (Eds.), *Future City Architecture for Optimal Living* (pp. 13–35). Basel: Springer.

Nature.com. (2006, August 10). Spotlight on Sendai. *Naturejobs.com* (Articles). Retrieved September 2, 2017, from https://www.nature.com/naturejobs/science/articles/10.1038/nj0122

Near Southside, Inc. (n/a). *Medical District* (Website). Retrieved September 15, 2017, from https://www.nearsouthsidefw.org/medical-district.html

Nisen, M. (2013, February 13). Mayo Clinic Has a Radical Plan to Expand Its Reach Across the World. *Business Insider*. Retrieved October 26, 2017, from http://www.businessinsider.com/mayo-clinic-ceo-future-of-healthcare-2013-2?r=US&IR=T&IR=T

Norões, L. (2016, May 11). Healthcare City—A New Innovation Ecosystem for the Healthcare Sector. *Portugal Startups.com*. Retrieved August 31, 2017, from http://portugalstartups.com/2016/05/healthcare-city-new-innovation-ecosystem-healthcare-sector/

Palti, I., & Bar, M. (2015, August 28). A Manifesto for Conscious Cities: Should Streets Be Sensitive to Our Mental Needs? *The Guardian*. Retrieved September 15, 2017, from https://www.theguardian.com/cities/2015/aug/28/manifesto-conscious-cities-streets-sensitive-mental-needs

Pofeldt, E. (2016, August 11). The Top Start-up Mecca in America Is Far from Silicon Valley. *CNBC.com*. Retrieved September 5, 2017, from https://www.cnbc.com/2016/08/11/austin-is-top-place-for-startups-in-america-not-silicon-valley.html

Polizer, M. (2017, February 27). Taking the Smart Route to Inclusive, Sustainable and Connected Cities. *Devex*. Retrieved August 28, 2017, from https://www.

devex.com/news/taking-the-smart-route-to-inclusive-sustainable-and-connected-cities-89444

Porter, M. E., & Lee, T. H. (2013, October). The Strategy that Will Fix Health Care. *Harvard Business Review 91*, 24–24.

Raghupathi, W., & Raghupathi, V. (2014). Big Data Analytics in Healthcare: Promise and Potential. *Health Information Science and Systems, 2*(3), 1–10.

Reisman, D. (2010). *Health Tourism: Social Welfare Through International Trade*. Cheltenham: Edward Elgar.

Retterath, M., Olsen, T., & Eliades, G. (2013, September 25). *Opportunities in Integrated Care for Pharma and Medtech* (Bain Brief). Bain & Company. Retrieved September 10, 2017, from http://www.bain.com/publications/articles/opportunities-in-integrated-care-for-pharma-and-medtech.aspx

Salomaa, K. (2015, March 6). *Tampere Health Village*. Health Spa at FinnMedi (Slideshare). Retrieved September 16, 2017, from https://www.slideshare.net/DeliaHealthSPA/finn-medi-healthvillage20150306

Schmid, H. (2009). *Economy of Fascination: Dubai and Las Vegas as Themed Urban Landscapes*. Berlin: Gebrüder Borntraeger.

Smith, M., & Kelly, C. (2006). Wellness Tourism. *Tourism Recreation Research, 31*(1), 1–4.

Smith, M., & Puczkó, L. (2009). *Health and Wellness Tourism* (2nd ed.). Oxford: Butterworth-Heinemann.

Stephano, R.-M., & Abratt, D. (2012, April 11). Jeju Healthcare Town Asia's New Medical Tourism Hub. *Medical Tourism Magazine*. Retrieved August 31, 2017, from http://www.medicaltourismmag.com/jeju-healthcare-town-asiaaes-new-medical-tourism-hub/

Suter, E., Oelke, N. D., Adair, C. E., & Armitage, G. D. (2009). Ten Key Principles for Successful Health Systems Integration. *Healthcare Quarterly, 13*(Spec. No.), 16–23.

Tokoro, N. (2016). *The Smart City and the Co-creation of Value: A Source of New Competitiveness in a Low-Carbon Society*. Tokyo: Springer Japan.

Van Gorder, C. (2015). Working Harder at Working Together: Building Collaboration Between Public Health and Health Care Delivery. *Frontiers in Public Health, 3*, 167.

V-cube. (n/a). *Kagawa Medical Association* (Customer's Case Studies). Retrieved August 28, 2017, from http://demomy.vcube.com/introduction/example/meeting/36.html

Visit Finland. (2016). *Suomesta hyvinvointimatkailun kärkimaa—25 suomalaistuotetta edustamaan Suomea hyvinvointimatkakohteena* [Finland as a Top Country in Wellbeing Tourism—25 Finnish Products to Represent Finland as a Well-Being Travel Destination]. Visit Finland, January 27, 2016. Retrieved September 16, 2017, from http://www.visitfinland.fi/news/suomesta-hyvinvointimatkailun-karkimaa/

Wang, L., & Alexander, C. A. (2015). Big Data in Medical Applications and Health Care. *Current Research in Medicine, 6*(1), 1–8.

White, V., & Harris, J. (Eds.). (2001). *Developing Good Practice in Community Care: Partnership and Participation*. London/Philadelphia: Jessica Kingsley Publishers.

Woodman, J. (2012). *Patients Beyond Borders: Dubai Healthcare City Edition*. Chapel Hill: Healthy Travel Media.

Yamada, K. (2017, March 19). Jeju Island Goes Green as Chinese Tourists Go Elsewhere. *Nikkei Asian Review*. Retrieved September 9, 2017, from https://asia.nikkei.com/Business/Trends/Jeju-Island-goes-green-as-Chinese-tourists-go-elsewhere

CHAPTER 7

Towards Inclusive Wellness City

Abstract This chapter broadens the discussion to the socio-economic context of urban economic development, beginning with the urban health divide, which is a serious socio-economic problem in practically all advanced countries. A corrective policy perspective on community health is referred to as wellness for all, a perspective that indirectly contributes to wellness-oriented economic development. The chapter ends by building a picture of wellness as a balancing and integrative factor in urban economic development, which widens the perspective from a narrow cluster policy to inclusive growth.

Keywords Health divide • Urban wellness • Community health • Integration • Inclusion • Inclusive growth

This section broadens the discussion towards critical views of wellness-related development policies conditioned by global economic restructuring, financial crises, and a host of other structural factors. One of the fundamental questions is the impact of global trends on a locality's ability to develop urban wellness and utilize local assets in wellness-oriented economic development. Another question worth pondering is how the two seemingly opposing perspectives on local wellness economy –people-oriented versus business-oriented—relate to each other. Our synthesizing

A.-V. Anttiroiko, *Wellness City*,
https://doi.org/10.1007/978-3-319-75562-5_7

approach emphasizes the need for inclusive and integrative wellness-oriented local economic development.

Urban Health Divide

As mentioned earlier, as an urban phenomenon a wellness city refers to structures and processes of an urban community that facilitate city dwellers' and visitors' pursuit of practicing health-promoting lifestyles in an integrated manner. Such a pursuit is considerably affected by global trends and conditioned by community characteristics. It is notable that the fruits of such local structural tendencies and facilitative processes are divided neither equally nor fairly between community members. Such an inequality has long historical roots, and while at global level there has been a decrease in inequality due to the rise of such countries as China and India, during the last thirty years or so post-industrial economies have become increasingly divided. Even in the wealthiest and most connected global cities economic inequalities have been on the rise (Hambleton 2015).

Economic inequalities and polarization have contributed to a striking *health divide*, both between rich and poor countries and between rich and poor within each country (e.g. Hero et al. 2017; Buchan et al. 2017). For example, in 2012 the top 5% of the US population ranked by their health care expenses were responsible for more than half of all health care spending and the top 50% of the population accounted for 97.3% of overall health care expenditures, which leaves only a tiny share to the rest (Cohen 2014).

This issue has a connection with local economic development. It translates into a question of how such health inequalities affect the local economy and the preconditions for local economic development. It is fair to say that economic polarization, social exclusion and dual city tendencies are not good for the economy or the aggregate well-being of any territorial community. Scholars have recently started to pay attention to social responsibility, smart growth, economic democracy, and inclusive prosperity, which are critical in building healthy connections between urban wellness and economic development.

The idea of *inclusive prosperity* entails that the opportunities and benefits of economic growth should be widely shared among all segments of society. At grassroots level urban areas continue to afford new opportunities to employees and businesses but are increasingly split between wealthy knowledge workers and low-paid service workers. Gentrification, economic segregation, and a disappearing middle class are symptoms of uneven progress on prosperity that are not that uncommon, especially among major cities in the Western world. In other words, we are facing a problem of low attainment of inclusive growth in metropolitan cities, which self-evidently reduces chances to tackle the health divide (Florida and McLean 2017; Shearer et al. 2017; Shearer and Berube 2017).

While in past centuries density was associated with community health risks and problems, it is undeniable that today the populations living in larger cities in the developed world are healthier than their respective national average. Cities stay healthy and become even healthier if they are able to reinforce health-creating aspects of urban life—fewer cars, fewer guns, better social inclusion, smarter regulations, efficient urban informatics, great hospitals, and a culture of wellness—and thus counterbalance not only the disease-spreading consequences of high population density (Glaeser 2012) but also the inherent risks of urban life in late modernity (Beck 1992; Zinn 2008).

Wellness for All

The fundamental issue here is whether we should take a holistic-inclusive or instrumental-individualistic view of wellness in urban development. An *inclusive view* aims for a balance between community health and economic development, while an *instrumental view* approaches wellness professionally within a conventional cluster policy agenda. The former is dedicated to finding synergies between social and economic processes under a wellness theme, thus taking a broad view of the utilization of local assets and a look at spreading benefits as fairly and widely as possible among the members of the community. This setting is illustrated in Fig. 7.1 by presenting two ideal types, individualist (neoliberal) and collectivistic (welfarist) views of a wellness city policy.

Somewhere between the two ideal types is a kind of third way, responsible developmentalism, which builds on healthiness, inclusiveness, entrepreneurship, and integration in community development. Wellness-oriented economic development starts from *community health*. Its maximization requires the presence of strong social capital, public participation, a healthy environment, accessible services, and good governance (McMurray and Clendon 2015). Much the same can be said about urban economic development, for it requires that the urban setting as a whole supports such an endeavor and that the instrumental view of economic development is balanced by

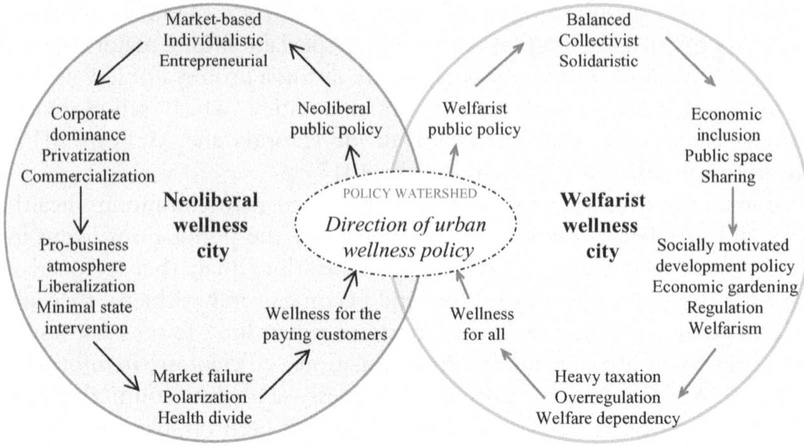

Fig. 7.1 Two ideal types of wellness city policy: neoliberalism versus welfarism

higher-level goals. Florida and McLean (2017) call such an approach urbanism-for-all. It goes beyond affordable housing and inclusionary zoning to facilitate accessibility among low-income communities. Their main message is the need to work on many fronts at the same time, in a focused manner, and with the diversity of stakeholder groups in mind. They describe the revitalization of the Union Market district in northeast Washington, DC, as a pilot area for testing practical policies and initiatives that are assumed to promote inclusive prosperity.

Union Terminal Market began as a food production and distribution hub in the 1930s. A new indoors market was built in 1967. The area started to show signs of decline in the 1980s. In 2009, the District published a framework for future development of the area. A few years later the developer Edens opened a new Union Market food hall and in the mid-2010s the first mixed residential/retail space was opened—to be followed by many new projects if the area development proved viable (Kashino 2015). The current revitalization process of the district has brought together community members and a range of experts and institutional stakeholders to help create an overall vision and an area plan, which eventually became an idea of transforming a former food production and distribution center into a *district forinclusive prosperity*. It boiled down to being a destination for retail, restaurants, arts, and culture, a forum for local events, a flexible workspace for businesses, and a lively residential area. The district needed to create jobs, engage the surrounding community, inspire connections between the existing neighborhood and the broader city, preserve historical identity, and incubate entrepreneurship—all this while making local property development economically viable (Florida and McLean 2017). The key point here is that inclusive prosperity has a significant integrative and balancing role in the development of an area.

For most small and middle-sized cities, high-profile investment and attraction strategies are not necessarily viable options. They need to build on their local assets, including local social capital and entrepreneurship. The restructuring process of Littleton, a suburb of Denver, Colorado, is as a good learning case in this respect. The story began in the late 1980s, at a time when the municipality lost a missile manufacturer (currently known as Lockheed Martin), which laid off almost 8000 people in all. This "rocket town" needed to restructure its economy and find replacement jobs for thousands of workers. The key figure in this story is Chris Gibbons, Littleton's business director at that time, who, with his team, collaborated with a Denver-based think tank, the Center for the New West, which was anxious to test a theory developed by MIT economist David Birch (1979, 1987). According to this theory, so-called Stage 2 companies (employing between 10 and 100 people and with an annual revenue of at least USD 1 million) create the best kind of jobs for middle-class workforces. Such companies could drive a local economy upward. Littleton started to identify local Stage 2 companies and offered them resources to help expand their business. Over the following 25 years, Littleton's population increased by one-quarter but the number of jobs tripled and the city's sales tax revenue grew dramatically. Gibbons called such a policy *economic gardening*. He later helped to set up the National Center for Economic Gardening. hosted by the Michigan-based Edward Lowe Foundation (Farmer 2014).

Another important idea is that of creating new and better jobs by developing spaces and programs to incubate entrepreneurs. Supporting entrepreneurship is an effective way to connect with the surrounding community. Most scalable startups are typically in high-tech and creative industries, but many low-tech startup models can grow and develop in spaces such as that described in the case of the revitalization of Union Market (Florida and McLean 2017). This is where the community and entrepreneurship generate synergies and the case of Union Market is illuminating, for there the boundaries between visitor and vendor spaces are intentionally blurred, fostering a feeling of community between all participants. In addition, flexible, multi-purpose venues such as Dock 5 and Lab 1270 host a wide array of events, forums, and activities that naturally bring diverse groups together to share ideas. This points to the significance of "third places" in a city (Oldenburg 1989), which, as the sites of consumption, interaction, and sociability, are increasingly fusing with the "second places," or sites of work and production (Florida and McLean 2017).

A wellness sector has a lot to offer *urban revitalization* projects. As a first instance, this appears in the form of lifestyle boutiques, beauty shops, hair salons, small-scale spas, therapeutic massage services, elderly care clinics, wellness clinics, and healthcare kiosks. Its role can, however, be more profound than just offering a few shops or clinics. Thus, as a second instance, wellness can be an integral part of the philosophy of urban revitalization. It can give a sense of pride, caring, and social inclusion, and strengthen belief in the potential of the community to provide better living conditions and amenities for local residents. Sometimes only one successful center can have a dramatic influence on the sense of place, help to attract investments, and improve employment. This happened, for example, with the establishment of the Stephen Klein Wellness Center in March 2015, in a weary neighborhood in Philadelphia where residents are nearly twice as likely to live in extreme poverty as people elsewhere in the city, where the unemployment rate is twice the city's average, and where domestic violence, child neglect, and homelessness are part of daily life for many. A large part of the population went without health care and were mainly served by the emergency room. The wellness center was an intervention in such local conditions, it provided healthcare facilities—primary care, behavioral health, dental care, and a pharmacy—plus activities and services such as the YMCA, stress reduction and yoga classes, a food pantry, and a teaching kitchen with occasional cooking demonstrations. The idea was to offer integrated care, which made the center an important player in the local community (PHFA n/a).

Wellness as a Balancing and Integrative Factor

Creating an inclusive, enabling, and empowering wellness city has a better chance of supporting wellness cluster development than a narrowly focused instrumental cluster policy scheme. This highlights the special nature of wellness, which has an inherent human and community connection that offers a unique chance for *business-community integration*.

A serious attempt to achieve inclusive prosperity and growth is an important premise for the development of a wellness economy. Some critical aspects of such a growth scheme have been identified by Shearer and Berube (2017) on the basis of their analysis of the inclusiveness of growth in selected US metropolises (*Metro Monitor*). They concluded that cities with inclusive growth shared a few common traits that have obvious connections with wellness cluster development:

1) Cities that achieved inclusive growth tended to add jobs in internationally exposed traded sectors—such as advanced business and professional services, information, and manufacturing—at a faster rate than the rest of the nation. In a wellness cluster, this point relates to Wellness++ or wellness-related research and technology, which is an important part of a growing wellness sector. The other important sector is professional IT-assisted health care and medical wellness services. The former belong to a super-creative core, while the latter to creative professionals in Florida's classification of the occupations of the creative class (Florida 2002).
2) Inclusive cities tended to add jobs in lower-paid types of work within the traded sectors, that is, in the traded sectors cited above hiring seemed to be skewed in favor of middle- or low-skilled workers. This hints that there may be employment opportunities in selected niches for wellness-related middle- and low-skill occupations.
3) Inclusive cities balanced traded-sector job growth with growth in well-paying jobs for middle-skilled workers in non-traded sectors such as construction, logistics, and health care. This emphasizes the role of health care and its business potential through expansion, outsourcing, restructuring, and service integration.
4) Inclusive cities relied on traded and secondary sectors to fuel modest growth of typically local-serving sectors such as hospitality and retail that do not pay well, but expand employment opportunities for less-skilled workers. This is an important point. Wellness may have a special role as an internally diverse, easy-entry cluster in improving inclusion in local labor markets.

The *Metro Monitor* suggests that real progress towards inclusive growth requires an informed and intentional approach, one that leverages metropolitan assets around innovation and trade to support sectors that can provide appealing opportunities for the greatest number of workers who, by and large, belong to the creative class (Florida 2002). At a first glance, inclusive growth seems to favor a "high-road" economic development strategy that prioritizes both high-skill and middle-skill traded sectors. However, it was actually only after hiring in low-paid sectors that real improvements in inclusion outcomes materialized (Shearer and Berube 2017). A vital part of traditional non-tradable sectors—health care, education, hospitality, retail, and construction—can be made tradable under certain conditions. This may be of particular relevance if it helps to increase the attractiveness of the local or regional economy, improve the flexibility and fluidity in the local labor market, acquire capital and talent for the city, and create synergistic, mutually supportive, interindustry relations.

Finally, it is good to remember the question raised by Charles Montgomery: if economic freedom and high income is a precondition for subjective well-being, why have we not experienced an immense surge in happiness in wealthy Western economies? This urges us to ask new questions about the consequences of economic polarization and about the connection between material and mental well-being. There is something bigger that relates to quality of life and well-being that is at stake. At community level we can talk of "happy cities," which are in the making in different parts of the world through urban innovations that transform people's lives. It invites us to take a new look at the places where we spend most of our lives and ask straightforwardly if our city is a place that makes us happy (Montgomery 2015). A wellness for all policy has the potential to serve as a link between thriving urban economy and happiness.

References

Beck, U. (1992). *Risk Society: Towards a New Modernisation*. London: Sage.

Birch, D. L. (1979). *The Job Generation Process. MIT Program on Neighborhood and Regional Change*. Cambridge: MIT Program on Neighborhood and regional Change.

Birch, D. L. (1987). *Job Creation in America*. New York: Free Press.

Buchan, I. E., Kontopantelis, E., Sperrin, M., Chandola, T., & Doran, T. (2017). North-South Disparities in English Mortality 1965–2015: Longitudinal Population Study. *Journal of Epidemiology & Community Health, 71*(9), 928–936.

Cohen, S. B. (2014, October). *The Concentration of Health Care Expenditures and Related Expenses for Costly Medical Conditions, 2012* (Statistical Brief #455). MEPS, Medical Expenditure Panel Survey. Retrieved August 30, 2017, from https://meps.ahrq.gov/data_files/publications/st455/stat455.pdf

Farmer, L. (2014, June 27). Economic Gardening Is Growing, but What Is It? *Governing*. Retrieved August 30, 2017, from http://www.governing.com/topics/finance/gov-how-to-grow-businesses-that-grow-the-economy.html

Florida, R. (2002). *The Rise of the Creative Class: And How It's Transforming Work, Leisure, Community and Everyday Life*. New York: Perseus Book.

Florida, R., & McLean, J. W. (2017, July 11). What Inclusive Urban Development Can Look Like. *Harvard Business Review*. Retrieved August 29, 2017, from https://hbr.org/2017/07/what-inclusive-urban-development-can-look-like

Glaeser, E. (2012). *Triumph of the City: How Our Greatest Invention Makes Us Richer, Smarter, Greener, Healthier and Happier*. New York: Penguin.

Hambleton, R. (2015). *Leading the Inclusive City: Place-Based Innovation for a Bounded Planet*. Bristol: Policy Press.

Hero, J. O., Zaslavsky, A. M., & Blendon, R. J. (2017). The United States Leads Other Nations in Differences by Income in Perceptions of Health and Health Care. *Health Affairs, 36*(6), 1032–1040.

Kashino, M. M. (2015, April 20). The Union Market Housing Boom Is About to Explode. *Washingtonian*. Retrieved December 3, 2017, from https://www.washingtonian.com/2015/04/20/the-union-market-housing-boom-is-about-to-explode/

McMurray, A., & Clendon, J. (2015). *Community Health and Wellness: Primary Health Care in Practice* (5th ed.). Chatswood: Elsevier.

Montgomery, C. (2015). *Happy City: Transforming Our Lives Through Urban Design*. London: Penguin Books.

Oldenburg, R. (1989). *The Great Good Place: Cafes, Coffee Shops, Community Centers, Beauty Parlors, General Stores, Bars, Hangouts, and How They Get You Through the Day*. New York: Paragon House.

PHFA. (n/a). *Bringing a Healing Touch. Community Revitalization*. Harrisburg: The Pennsylvania Housing Finance Agency. Retrieved August 30, 2017, from http://www.phfa.org/forms/success_stories/community_revitalization/bringing_a_healing_touch.pdf

Shearer, R., & Berube, A. (2017, April 27). *The Surprisingly Short List of US Metro Areas Achieving Inclusive Economic Growth*. Brookings, The Avenue. Retrieved August 29, 2017, from https://www.brookings.edu/blog/the-avenue/2017/04/27/the-surprisingly-short-list-of-u-s-metro-areas-achieving-inclusive-economic-growth/

Shearer, R., Friedhoff, A., Shah, I., & Berube, A. (2017, March). *Metro Monitor: An Index of Inclusive Economic Growth in the 100 Largest U.S. Metropolitan Areas*. Metropolitan Policy Program at Brookings. Washington, DC: Brookings. Retrieved August 29, 2017, from https://www.brookings.edu/wp-content/uploads/2017/02/metro-monitor_full_af2.pdf

Zinn, J. O. (Ed.). (2008). *Social Theories of Risk and Uncertainty: An Introduction*. Oxford: Blackwell.

CHAPTER 8

Conclusion

Abstract The brief concluding chapter provides a summary of this book on wellness cities at the intersection of holistic health, economy, and urban governance. It highlights the main message, summarizes the role of the eight dimensions of the Y model of wellness, and identifies six possible roles for wellness in local economic development. The discussion ends with remarks on the relevance of demand-side and supply-side strategies, the governing capacity needed in the promotion of a wellness city, and the need to support inclusive prosperity while developing a wellness city.

Keywords Wellness city • Local economic development • Governing capacity • Cluster policy

Previous chapters have shed light on various aspects of a wellness city and its utilization in local economic development. The concept of a wellness city apparently has two main conceptual components. The first, *wellness*, is a multi-dimensional, process-oriented concept rooted in personal choices of and responsibility for holistic health, manifest in a health-promoting lifestyle. To concretizing this phenomenon, this book presents a Y model of wellness as a crystallization of its major dimensions. The other component, the *city*, refers to a dense urban settlement that provides a context for wellness. As their synthesis, *urban wellness* captures an idea of urban community that, in an integrated manner, facilitates the city dweller's pursuit of a health-promoting lifestyle that aims at their holistic well-being.

A.-V. Anttiroiko, *Wellness City*,
https://doi.org/10.1007/978-3-319-75562-5_8

From urban wellness we take a step towards a particular activity context, that of the *economic development policy*. This is how wellness is perceived by those involved in local business, investment, and tourism promotion. From this point of view, the concept of a *wellness city* refers to policies and actions that, through the promotion of a wellness industry, improve the conditions for economic growth, community value generation, and business opportunity enhancement.

The eight dimensions of the Y model of wellness point to following special features to be taken into account in promoting a wellness cluster (see Fig. 8.1):

- Health is an undivided sector, within which *medical and wellness paradigms* should be fused in mutually supportive ways. Attention should generally be shifted from curative to preventive care, and from a medical to an holistic view of human health. Wellness, together with medicine and a health care system, form a huge economic sector, referred to in this book as Wellness+. The basic forms of generating wellness businesses in this field are service expansion, integration, restructuring, and outsourcing.
- *Spa, beauty, and fitness* are important urban amenities and benefit from service integration. They form a business in their own right, as seen in the mushrooming presence of spas, wellness and fitness centers, and beauty salons.

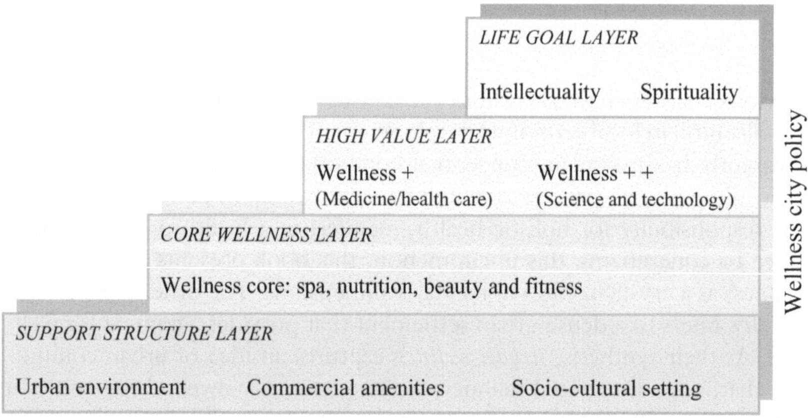

Fig. 8.1 Layers of a wellness city policy

- *Entertainment and shopping* form an amenity base that supports well-being; they are increasingly wellness-specific through wellness-oriented retail businesses and consumption-driven wellness destinations.
- *Nature and urban environments,* including wellness real estate, have the potential to increase local attractiveness and to create wellness communities and destinations with both natural assets and wellness-inspired urban design as attractions.
- *Health and wellness-related science, technology, and manufacturing* as a whole form a large segment in internationally tradable industries, referred to as Wellness++. From the point of view of locality development, the major manifestations are industrial, innovation, and service districts.
- *Intellectuality* relates to knowledge processes, innovation capability, and knowledge institutions that support urban wellness. Such processes can be facilitated via knowledge centers and participatory innovation platforms.
- *Culture and sociability* can be facilitated by various socio-cultural spaces, from "third places" to theme parks. Their dynamic aspect relates to eventification—including wellness festivals—as well as to virtual environments, which are likely to change the shape of urban wellness in the future.
- *Spirituality, meditation, and transcendence* form an activity area that creates value through mindfulness retreats, meditation centers, spiritual destinations, pilgrimages, and famous cemeteries.

The internal diversity of a wellness cluster is a reflection of the multi-dimensionality of holistic health. It hints at the multiple ways wellness can contribute to local economic development, depending on local conditions and strategic choices. We can identify six overlapping roles for wellness in local economic development:

- *Wellness as a target cluster*: For a city with good preconditions for utilizing various dimensions of wellness in its economic development, wellness can become one of the target clusters promoted by the city government and local business community.
- *Wellness as a set of priorities or spearhead industries*: Some wellness-related industries can spearhead industrial restructuring or urban revitalization; for example, wellness technology, medical tourism, or a spa industry.

- *Wellness in policy and service integration*: Wellness has various intersections and inter-sectoral interfaces with other policy areas, which provide opportunities for a wellness-oriented integration of services and development activities. The most significant being with the health care sector, but can also cover social, education, youth, sports, and cultural policies.
- *Wellness as a facilitative resource*: Wellness forms a generic support factor for local economic development in such areas as intellectuality, culture, amenitization, and natural and built environments.
- *Wellness in destination development*: Wellness provides opportunities to utilize historic and spiritual sites and local traditions in place promotion; and to invest in commercial wellness centers and tourist destinations to generate business, income, and jobs through consumption.
- *Wellness in eventification*: Wellness can be a unifying theme for various kinds of events, such as wellness or fitness festivals and religious events. Such a development has the potential to improve the image of a city, increase urban vitality, and to claim a city's share of event tourism.

Each city has its own history, characteristics, economic potential, and governing capacity, which implies that the role of wellness in local economic development must be assessed case by case. Growth in a global market does not tell an individual city government whether wellness should be its target cluster or what particular areas of urban wellness it should develop. *Local asset analysis* is a tool that can be used for assessing the preconditions for wellness-oriented economic development. If, in absolute or relational terms, the city has good preconditions for developing a wellness industry, the next step is to analyze this option against chosen cluster policy criteria (jobs, salary levels, location quotient, growth rates, etc.) and then to integrate major wellness destinations into community-wide development efforts.

One of the strategic choices is how the city positions itself as a *dissipative structure* and attempts to benefit from the flows of the wellness economy. The demand-side emphasis builds on local assets supported by extra-local resources to attract medical and wellness tourists or some other target groups to the city. Supply-side orientation is typical in innovation and export-oriented producer cities, each having their own economic specialties. They may have strengths in attracting and combining factors of production—capital, labor, talent, ideas, and entrepreneurship—to generate innovative wellness products, services, or technological systems to be exported to global markets.

Another critical issue is the *institutional orchestration* and *governance* of such an endeavor. A development project may be a nationally supported large-scale project, a local government-sponsored project, a partnership-based venture, or a purely privately organized project. This determines whether funding is primarily public or private, how risks are covered, and to what extent institutions of public governance intervene in the process.

Lastly, in this book we have emphasized the need for *inclusive urban wellness* as a precondition for optimal use of local resources and for achieving inclusive economic growth. Inclusive, enabling, and empowering wellness cities have the best chance of supporting wellness cluster development. This stresses an inherent human and community dimension of urban wellness. Wellness may be a high value-adding target cluster spearheaded by health and wellness technologies, R&D, and innovation, together with well-paying jobs in the health care sector, but it can also be built on locally rooted care, hospitality, and retail businesses with lower skill requirements and easy market entry. The latter is, in fact, an important aspect of urban vitality and a practical precondition for making a city genuinely inclusive.

The idea of a *wellness city* encourages local politicians, developers, entrepreneurs, and civic leaders to take a broad view of holistic health and its potential to harness local economic development. Wellness is a genuinely heterogeneous group of interrelated industries that, as a development concept, comprises diverse forms of activities, from wellness products to services, events, micro environments, full-service destinations, and urban design. It has the potential to be a high-profile target cluster or a supportive and integrative thematic cluster, depending upon the preconditions and economic profile of each city. Wellness as a whole has become a viable industry or economic cluster, which not only increases local prosperity but also connects this endeavor to social inclusion, sustainability, and the sense of community, which are critical to our endeavors to create the conditions for a better life for all.

Index

A.-V. Anttiroiko, *Wellness City*,
https://doi.org/10.1007/978-3-319-75562-5

W

Y

The manufacturer's authorised representative in the EU is Springer Nature Customer Service Centre GmbH, Europaplatz 3, 69115 Heidelberg, Germany. If you have any concerns regarding our products, please contact ProductSafety@springernature.com

Printed and bound by CPI Group (UK) Ltd, Croydon, CR0 4YY

30/09/2026

02225609-0017